Sides

ALSO BY MELICIA PHILLIPS

Working a Duck (with Sean McElroy)

Sides

OVER 150 ENTICING ACCOMPANIMENTS
THAT MAKE THE MEAL

By MELICIA PHILLIPS

CLARKSON POTTER / PUBLISHERS

NEW YORK

Published by Clarkson Potter/Publishers, 201 East 50th Street, New York, New York 10022. Member of the Crown Publishing Group.

Random House, Inc. New York, Toronto, London, Sydney, Auckland

CLARKSON N. POTTER, POTTER, and colophon are trademarks of Clarkson N. Potter, Inc.

Manufactured in the United States of America

Design by Margaret Hinders

Library of Congress Cataloging-in-Publication Data
Phillips, Melicia.
Sides : over 150 enticing accompaniments that make the meal / by Melicia
Phillips.—1st ed.
Includes index.
1. Side dishes (Cookery) I. Title
TX740.P47 1995
641.8′1—dc 20   94-28412
                                                                CIP

ISBN 0-517-59687-3

10   9   8   7   6   5   4   3   2   1

First Edition

Acknowledgments

To begin with, I would like to thank my agent, Carla Glasser, for helping me get this project off the ground. I would also like to thank my friend Bernadette for coming up with the idea in the first place and for trying out some of the recipes. My friend Sean deserves thanks for eating and commenting on a great many of the tested recipes. Finally I would like to thank Pam Krauss, my editor, for all her work and suggestions on *Sides*.

Contents

Introduction

After years of fielding questions and giving cooking advice to friends, family, and clients in the various New York restaurants where I worked, I began to notice the most common queries I received were for side dish ideas and preparations. I realized that many of the people I spoke with already knew what they were serving for a main course but needed inspiration for accompaniments. They wanted something to make the meal more exciting, more interesting—*different*.

Let's face it, the majority of American households have a repertoire of familiar standbys when it comes to making dinner: roast chicken, roast or grilled beef, pork chops, hamburgers, spaghetti, maybe a piece of fish. It's comforting to prepare the dishes one is familiar with and these favorites all share the advantage of being rather easy to make. However, variety *is* the spice of life, and we need it, even if the change is as small as serving a new potato dish. Sautéed chicken cutlets are quick and simple to prepare, but serve them with a baked potato and string beans every time, and you'll soon be bored. Substitute Curried Couscous with Pine Nuts and Currants for the potato and Sautéed Escarole with Garlic and Lemon for the string beans and you have a new beginning.

This is exactly how I think when I devise a new restaurant menu. I start by knowing that guests will expect choices based on chicken, beef, fish, or shellfish. I also know that many of the same people have been coming to the restaurant for months or even years and I have to create a new menu that will keep them coming back, even though I am still cooking chicken, beef, fish, or shellfish. One of my tricks for a successful restaurant menu is to entice people with sides. Say the word "fritter" and you're in! As a chef, I also want to cook well-rounded meals; my guests should feel that they have not only enjoyed a delicious dish but also eaten a few vegetables. I feel it is more interesting and thoughtful dining if each dish has sides tailored just for it, to complement and set off the entrée.

Frankly, it's more fun to eat vegetables if something has been "done" to them. This is not to say that a side must be complicated to be good. I've gotten more compliments for my simple Turnip Gratin, made essentially with three ingredients, than just about any other side dish I've ever made. Confident cooks know that simplicity is often best and that a recipe need not have a plenitude of ingredients to impress.

When choosing side dishes to serve with your entrée, there are several factors to take into consideration. To begin with, there is the element of style. The side dish should reflect the mood of the meal. Are you serving hamburgers and hot dogs at an outdoor barbecue or having a more formal meal? If the entrée is an elaborate preparation or composed of complex flavors, you may not want a complicated side dish; something more straightforward might show off your entrée to better advantage. Conversely, if the entrée is quite simple, you have the option of serving an equally uncomplicated side dish to retain the effect (as with a steak and baked potato) or putting more effort into your sides to elevate the meal to something a bit more special.

Then, of course, there are the issues of taste and texture to consider. The side dish should enhance and complement the main course in an organic way. If your entrée has a cream sauce, for example, your side probably should not, as it would create too rich a combination. Think instead of a side dish that would benefit from sopping up the cream sauce. Similarly, a starchy main course obviously doesn't need a starchy accompaniment. All flavors on the plate should harmonize, not clash.

Texture plays an important role as well. A crunchy entrée might do better with a creamy or puréed side rather than one of similar texture. A soft, delicate fish needs an accompaniment of firmer texture rather than a purée, so that everything is not just mush in the mouth. A meal of alternating textures makes more interesting dining and holds your attention longer.

Color is to be considered, too. It has often been said that we eat first with our eyes, and it's true. A plate full of beige food is not nearly as appealing as one with bright green and orange. After considering all the other factors relevant to deciding what you want to make, let color influence you as well.

Finally, let yourself be guided by what you are in the mood for. Do you have a craving for potatoes or pasta? Do you love greens? Do you want something creamy? Is there something in the refrigerator that needs to be used? Common sense as to what makes a balanced meal, combined with the above recommendations, should put you on the right track. However, when it really comes down to it, you should just consult your own tastes and desires. So what if everything on the plate is beige if that's what you want?

Creativity in the kitchen is assisted by two things: (1) having a well-stocked pantry and (2) not having one. Cooking can be much more pleasurable if some staples are kept in the house. Having a small stash of dried grains and legumes, cornmeal, and pasta can help put together a meal in no time. On the other hand, searching the refrigerator and cabinets for something to eat, finding half a bag of barley, or a few onions, can lead to some wonderful creations too. The important thing is to cook without fear.

Vegetable Sides

No meal is complete without a vegetable side dish, and, in fact, with meat playing a smaller role in many people's diets, the vegetable dish is often the star of the meal. Plain steamed or sautéed vegetables are fine from a nutritional standpoint, but the naturally appealing flavors of vegetables is even more enticing when something creative has been done with them. Sprinkling some herbs into a quick sauté or using bits of ham as a seasoning can add a whole new dimension to a dish. Combining vegetables for roasting and sautéing also makes for more interesting dining. Sometimes, changing a cooking technique turns an ordinary vegetable into something different, as when endive is braised in chicken stock rather than served raw in a salad. These twists give new life to familiar vegetables and can give you a new outlook on your favorite ingredients.

Sautéed Mushrooms with Oregano ◆ Tomatoes Stuffed with Basmati Rice ◆ Provençal Broiled Tomatoes ◆ Asparagus with Lemon Herb Butter ◆ Asparagus Almandine ◆ Corn, Red Pepper, and Green Bean Sauté ◆ Sweet and Spicy Okra and Rice ◆ Sugar Snaps with Mint Gremolata ◆ Snow Pea Parallelograms with Shiitakes ◆ Petits Pois with Ham and Mint ◆ Slow-Braised Red Cabbage ◆ Cabbage with Caraway and Bacon ◆ Baked Acorn Squash ◆ Zucchini Bateaux ◆ Pickled Onions ◆ Braised Leeks ◆ Baked Stuffed Onions ◆ Spicy Gingered Carrots ◆ Brussels Sprouts with Brown Butter and Pecans ◆ Rosemary-Scented Roasted Carrots, Turnips, and Shallots ◆ Braised Baby Bok Choy ◆ Glazed Endive ◆ Sautéed Escarole with Garlic and Lemon ◆ Braised Endive ◆ Chinese-Style Glazed Watercress ◆ Vegetable Quinoa ◆ Fried Rice with Spring Vegetables ◆ Baked Potato Stuffed with Cabbage and Mushrooms ◆ Potato Ragout with Red Wine and Wild Mushrooms

Sautéed Mushrooms with Oregano

This is simple and quick to prepare, and you can really use just about any herb you want. Oregano is especially good with mushrooms and gives them the right flavor to serve with pasta and tomato sauce dishes, veal, sausages, grilled steak, and seafood. If you've never tried fresh oregano, you'll find it much different from the dried version.

Try either Winter Vegetable Purée with Sweet Spices and Crispy Shallots (page 40) or steamed spinach (page 130) as a second side dish.

1 10-ounce box cultivated button mushrooms	**Salt and freshly ground pepper to taste**
1 tablespoon olive oil	**1 teaspoon coarsely chopped fresh oregano**
½ teaspoon minced garlic	**Squeeze of fresh lemon juice**

Trim the ends of the mushroom stems. Wipe each mushroom with a damp paper towel to remove any dirt. Slice them into ¼-inch pieces.

Heat the olive oil in a 10-inch sauté pan over high heat. When it just begins to smoke, add the mushrooms and sauté rapidly, tossing frequently. Sauté the mushrooms until they are browned, 3 to 5 minutes.

Lower the heat a bit and add the garlic. Continue sautéing, tossing occasionally, for another minute.

Season with salt and pepper. Add the oregano, toss to incorporate it, and then add a squeeze of lemon. Sauté another 30 seconds and serve.

Yield: 2 servings

Tomatoes Stuffed with Basmati Rice

Basmati rice is of Indian origin and is a long-grain aromatic variety. You can use any long-grain rice for this recipe, but if you've never had the pleasure of inhaling the distinctive fragrance of basmati rice, it's definitely worth seeking out. This is also a good way of using leftover cooked rice.

Some steamed spinach would be beautiful on the plate next to these tomatoes.

½ cup uncooked basmati rice

¾ cup cold water

1 large firm-fleshed tomato

2 teaspoons unsalted butter

1 scallion, thinly sliced

Pinch of saffron (about ⅛ teaspoon)

Salt and freshly ground pepper to taste

Preheat the oven to 375° F.

Combine the rice and water in a small saucepan. Bring to a boil over high heat, then reduce the heat as low as it will go and cover. Cook undisturbed for 20 minutes. Remove from the heat.

While the rice is cooking, cut the tomato in half crosswise. Using a sharp paring knife, carve out the center of each half. Discard the liquid and seeds but coarsely chop the firm pulp you have removed from the center.

In an 8-inch skillet, melt the butter over medium-low heat. Add the scallion, chopped tomato pulp, saffron, cooked rice, and salt and pepper. Sauté gently for 2 to 3 minutes, until everything is hot. Be careful not to burn the saffron.

Mound the rice mixture in the two tomato halves. Place them on a lightly greased sheet pan or pie plate and cover loosely with foil. Bake until heated through and the tomato is cooked, 20 to 30 minutes.

Yield: 2 servings

Provençal Broiled Tomatoes

These are a simple, delightful accent to a summertime meal. Perfect with grilled foods, especially steak but also hearty fish like tuna or swordfish, this dish is a good way to show off ripe tomatoes.

1 teaspoon minced shallot

¼ teaspoon minced garlic

¼ teaspoon dried sage

1 teaspoon dried thyme

1 anchovy

Salt and freshly ground pepper to taste

2 teaspoons olive oil

3 ripe medium tomatoes

Dry bread crumbs, for sprinkling

Combine the shallot, garlic, sage, thyme, anchovy, salt, pepper, and olive oil in a small bowl. Mash together to form a paste.

Cut the tomatoes in half crosswise and then trim the bottom of each half, so they will stand upright. Top each half with about ½ teaspoon of the herb mixture, spreading it all over the cut surface. Sprinkle each with about ½ teaspoon of bread crumbs. Arrange the tomatoes in a broiling pan without crowding and broil for 3 to 5 minutes, until they are hot and browned on top. Serve immediately.

Yield: 3 to 6 servings

Asparagus with Lemon Herb Butter

This is a simple way to serve asparagus, one that doesn't cloak the taste of spring.

½ pound thin asparagus

2 tablespoons fresh lemon juice

3 tablespoons cold, unsalted
  butter, cut into small pieces

Salt and freshly ground pepper to taste

1 teaspoon chopped mixed fresh
  herbs, such as parsley, chives,
  thyme, and/or chervil

Bend each piece of asparagus and let the stalk snap at its natural breaking point. Trim the stalks so they are all the same length. Peel the asparagus stems gently with a vegetable peeler. Save the trimming to make Herbed Asparagus Timbale (page 107) or for a soup.

Blanch the asparagus in lightly salted boiling water until just barely done and still crunchy, about 1 minute. Drain and arrange it on a warmed serving platter and keep warm.

In a small sauté pan, bring the lemon juice to a boil over high heat and cook it until it is reduced to less than a tablespoon—be careful not to let it brown. Take the pan off the heat and swirl in the butter, bit by bit, until the sauce thickens and has the level of tartness you like. You may not need all the butter.

Season the sauce with the salt, pepper, and the chopped herbs. Pour it immediately over the asparagus and serve.

Yield: 2 servings

Asparagus Almandine

Almandine is a classic and delicious preparation. I cook vegetables or fish in this manner when I want to make something very nice, yet also want something that won't cover up the true flavors of the food I am preparing. It is perfect for asparagus, which is often best simply steamed.

½ **pound thin asparagus**	**Salt and freshly ground pepper to**
1½ **tablespoons unsalted butter**	**taste**
¼ **cup blanched sliced almonds**	**1 tablespoon fresh lemon juice**
	1 teaspoon chopped fresh parsley

Trim the woody ends of each asparagus stalk. I do this by bending each stalk—it will naturally snap where the woody part ends. You can then trim the stalks to make them the same size. Peel each stalk lightly with a vegetable peeler. Save the trimmings for soup or Herbed Asparagus Timbale (page 107).

Blanch the asparagus in boiling salted water for about 1 minute, depending on how thick it is. Cook it until it is done but still crunchy. Drain the asparagus and arrange it on a warmed platter.

In a small sauté pan, melt the butter over medium-high heat. Add the sliced almonds and the salt and pepper. Cook the butter and almonds, swirling the pan, until the almonds take on a little color and the butter browns a bit. Quickly add the lemon juice and parsley and pour the almandine sauce over the asparagus. Serve immediately.

Yield: 2 servings

Corn, Red Pepper, and Green Bean Sauté

I like this dish for its color and versatility. Dicing the green beans and red pepper the same size as the corn kernels makes a great presentation. You can figure on getting about ½ cup of kernels from 1 ear of fresh corn. Serve it with a potato gratin (pages 36, 37, 38) or Egg Noodle Gratin (page 52).

¼ **pound green beans**	**1 cup corn kernels, fresh or**
1 small red bell pepper	**thawed frozen**
1½ **tablespoons olive oil**	**Salt and freshly ground pepper to**
	taste

Trim the green beans and slice them into ¼-inch pieces.

Trim the top off the pepper and cut the pepper in half. Remove the seeds and trim away the pith. Cut the pepper into ¼-inch strips and then cut it again crosswise into ¼-inch dice.

Heat the olive oil over high heat in a 10-inch sauté pan. Add the green beans, red pepper, and corn kernels. Sprinkle with salt and pepper and sauté, tossing, until the vegetables are just cooked, about 2 to 3 minutes. Serve immediately.

Yield: 2 servings

Sweet and Spicy Okra and Rice

Okra is one of those things that you either like or you don't. This preparation is highly seasoned and goes well with southern-style dishes like fried chicken, ham, or smothered pork chops. String beans would also work in this recipe.

1 tablespoon unsalted butter	Small pinch of ground cardamom
1 teaspoon minced garlic	1 cup chicken stock
¼ cup diced onion	⅛ teaspoon hot red pepper flakes
½ pound okra	Salt to taste
1 tablespoon honey	2 tablespoons uncooked long-grain
2 canned plum tomatoes, crushed	rice
¼ teaspoon ground cumin	Juice of ½ lemon

In a 1½-quart nonreactive saucepan, melt the butter over medium heat. Add the garlic and onion and cook, stirring occasionally, until they are soft and lightly browned—about 5 minutes or so.

Add the okra, honey, tomatoes, cumin, cardamom, chicken stock, hot red pepper flakes, and salt and stir to combine. Cover the pot and simmer over medium-low heat, stirring occasionally, for 1 hour. Add a bit of water to the okra, if necessary, to keep it moist during cooking.

Stir in the rice and re-cover the pot. Continue cooking until the rice is done, about 20 minutes. Season with the lemon juice and serve.

Yield: 2 to 4 servings

Sugar Snaps with Mint Gremolata

Gremolata is a seasoning mixture, traditionally made with parsley and served as a topping for osso buco. Mint gives it a nice twist, especially because it has a fondness for peas. This dish is pretty basic and not likely to clash with much—the mint gremolata just perks up the sugar snaps a bit. The gremolata is also good on fresh fava beans and snow peas.

2 teaspoons minced fresh mint	$\frac{1}{2}$ pound sugar snap peas, trimmed
$\frac{1}{2}$ teaspoon grated lemon zest	and strings removed
Scant $\frac{1}{2}$ teaspoon minced garlic	Salt to taste
2 teaspoons olive oil	

Combine the mint, lemon zest, and garlic in a small bowl and mix well.

Heat the olive oil in an 8-inch sauté pan over medium-high heat. Add the sugar snaps and sauté, tossing for 2 minutes, until they have turned bright green. Add the gremolata and salt, toss a few more times, and serve immediately.

Yield: 2 servings

Snow Pea Parallelograms with Shiitakes

Snow peas cook so quickly that they are a good choice for a delicious, no-fuss side dish. This fresh-tasting dish with earthy undertones would be just right with a simple meal of chicken breast or roast beef.

$\frac{1}{2}$ pound snow peas	$\frac{1}{2}$ teaspoon minced garlic
8 fresh shiitake mushrooms	1 teaspoon soy sauce
1 teaspoon vegetable oil	Salt to taste

String the snow peas and then cut each one crosswise into 3 pieces, holding your knife at a 45° angle, to form parallelograms.

Remove and discard the stems from the mushrooms and wipe the caps clean with a damp cloth. Cut the caps into quarters.

In a 10-inch sauté pan, heat the vegetable oil over medium heat. Add the quartered shiitakes and sauté, stirring frequently, until they are cooked through and lightly browned, about 3 minutes.

Add the garlic and snow peas and sauté another 2 minutes, until the snow peas are bright green, yet still crunchy. Season with the soy sauce and salt and serve immediately.

Yield: 2 to 4 servings

Petits Pois with Ham and Mint

This is a pretty little dish, all green and pink with fresh bright flavors. It is versatile and can be served with lots of entrées. I think of it as a summertime thing, and so it might be particularly nice with light fish dishes. Then again, little peas always go well with little birds.

Frozen peas are, in my experience, always better than the fresh ones I can get. In fact, they are really so good I don't hesitate to use them.

2 tablespoons unsalted butter	**1 10-ounce box frozen petits pois**
½ small onion, cut into tiny dice	**Salt and freshly ground pepper to**
½ teaspoon grated lemon zest	**taste**
2 ounces ham or Canadian bacon,	**1 teaspoon chopped fresh mint**
cut into pea-sized dice (about	
⅓ cup)	

In a small saucepan, melt the butter over low heat. Add the onion and lemon zest to the butter and cook them gently until the onion is soft, but not browned—about 3 minutes.

Add the ham or Canadian bacon to the saucepan and continue cooking gently for another minute. Add the peas to the pot and stir to combine and coat the peas with the butter. Season with salt and pepper and cook, stirring occasionally, for about 5 minutes or until the peas are hot. Add the mint, stir to combine, and serve immediately.

Yield: 4 servings

Slow-Braised Red Cabbage

This is one of those comfort foods that make you feel warm on a cold night. It's great with pork chops, but also with sausages, fried or roast chicken, and duck. Serve another side dish, like steamed carrots or broccoli, that will show off the color of the cabbage. And don't forget some potatoes.

2 strips lean bacon, cut into ¼-inch pieces	½ cup white wine vinegar
1 onion, peeled and sliced	1 cup chicken stock
4 cups shredded red cabbage	Salt and freshly ground pepper to taste

In a 2-quart saucepan, cook the bacon over medium heat until the fat has rendered and the bacon is crisp, about 5 minutes.

Add the onion slices and cook them in the bacon fat, stirring occasionally, until they are soft but not browned, about 5 minutes.

Add the cabbage, vinegar, and stock and stir to mix everything together. Bring to a boil, lower the heat to a simmer, and cook the cabbage, covered, for a half hour. Uncover the pot and continue cooking the cabbage, stirring occasionally, until it is mellow and soft, and the liquid has reduced somewhat, about 20 minutes longer. Season with salt and pepper.

Yield: 2 to 4 servings

NOTE: This dish keeps well in the refrigerator and is better if made a day or two ahead.

Cabbage with Caraway and Bacon

This delicious, gutsy side dish would be just right with pork, but also with chicken, duck, or other game birds. Try it with some plain boiled potatoes or Mushroom Strudel (page 98).

6 strips bacon, cut in ¾-inch pieces	2 tablespoons white wine vinegar
½ onion, sliced lengthwise	Salt and freshly ground pepper to taste
4 cups chopped cabbage, cut into 1-inch dice	½ teaspoon caraway seeds

Place the bacon in a 10-inch skillet and cook it over medium heat until crisp, about 10 minutes. Pour off all but 1 tablespoon of the fat.

Add the onion and cook 5 minutes, until it has softened.

Lower the heat to medium-low and add the cabbage, vinegar, salt, and pepper and stir everything together. Cook for 15 minutes, stirring occasionally. Add the caraway seeds and continue cooking until the cabbage has softened but still has a bit of crunch, about another 5 to 10 minutes. Taste and adjust the seasonings.

Yield: 2 to 4 servings

Baked Acorn Squash

Baked squash is a simple side dish to prepare and one that can be varied easily. Many hard squash lend themselves to this preparation, and you can change the flavors in the butter, using herbs, chili, curry, or other spices.

Squash is a fall vegetable, so I like to serve it with dishes appropriate to that season. Duck, game, and turkey are all good candidates, as well as the usual chicken, pork, lamb, or beef.

Serve a dark leafy green alongside this squash, such as Kale with Bacon and Onion (page 127) or Creamed Spinach (page 129).

2 tablespoons unsalted butter	**Salt and freshly ground pepper**
1 teaspoon minced garlic	**to taste**
¼ teaspoon ground cumin	**1 acorn squash, cut in half and**
A few gratings of nutmeg	**seeded**
Tiny pinch of cayenne pepper	

Preheat the oven to 375°F.

Place 1 tablespoon of the butter, ½ teaspoon garlic, ⅛ teaspoon cumin, nutmeg, cayenne, salt, and pepper in each squash cavity. Roast for 50 to 60 minutes or until a fork easily pierces the flesh. Serve immediately.

Yield: 2 servings

Zucchini Bateaux

Literally, this means "zucchini boats," because when the zucchini is halved and then hollowed out it resembles a boat. You can also hollow out a whole zucchini to form zucchini canoes.

These can be a rather elegant side dish to serve alongside meats or the more hearty fish. Entrées with sauces flavored with tomatoes, garlic, onions, olives, herbs like rosemary, thyme, or summer savory, and based on meat juices rather than cream are all suitable for pairing with Zucchini Bateaux. Depending on your entrée, Sautéed Mushrooms with Oregano (page 8) or Corn, Red Pepper, and Green Bean Sauté (page 12) would make a fine second side dish.

2 large zucchini	½ cup dry bread crumbs
2 tablespoons unsalted butter, plus	1 teaspoon chopped fresh thyme
additional 1 to 2 tablespoons	½ teaspoon salt
butter if desired	A few grinds of black pepper
3 garlic cloves, minced	1 tablespoon fresh lemon juice
1 shallot, minced	

Trim the zucchini, discarding the ends, and cut each zucchini crosswise into 3 pieces. Then cut each piece in half lengthwise. With a melon baller, carve a well in each piece, being careful not to go all the way through to the bottom. It's up to you whether you do this from the cut side or the green side—both ways look good. Finely chop the zucchini trimmings.

In a small skillet, melt the butter over medium-low heat. Add the garlic, shallot, and zucchini trimmings. Cook gently for about 5 minutes, until soft but not brown.

Preheat the oven to 375°F.

Place the cooked zucchini mixture in a bowl, add the bread crumbs, thyme, salt, pepper, and lemon juice and mix well. Taste and adjust the seasonings. The stuffing should be moist enough to hold together. If it is too dry, add a little soft butter.

Fill each zucchini boat with the stuffing, mounding it nicely. Place them on a lightly greased cookie sheet or in a shallow baking dish and bake for about a half hour. Test for doneness with the tip of a small knife—it should go in easily near the bottom of the boat. If the tops are not browned enough, run the boats under the broiler for a moment.

Yield: 4 to 6 servings

NOTE: The filled zucchini boats can be refrigerated overnight before baking if you wish.

Pickled Onions

Pickled onions, like caramelized garlic, are more of an accent than a true side dish, but they can add a lot to a meal. A few pieces of pickled onion next to a steak, for example, contribute a diversion for your palate, relieving it of the sameness of the meat. I also believe they aid in digestion.

You can use this pickling recipe to prepare other vegetables, such as shallots, carrots, or turnips.

3 medium onions	**4 teaspoons sugar**
1 tablespoon salt	**A few whole black peppercorns**
1½ cups white wine vinegar	**1 bay leaf**

Peel the onions and slice them as you wish—I slice them into ¼-inch half-moons.

Place a quart of water in a nonreactive container large enough to hold it and the onions. Dissolve the salt in the water to form a brine. Add the onions. Cover and refrigerate overnight.

Drain the onions. Place the vinegar, sugar, peppercorns, and bay leaf in a small nonreactive saucepan and bring to a boil. Pour the mixture over the onions (there should be enough to cover). Let cool, cover, and refrigerate for 24 hours. The onions are now ready to be eaten. They can remain immersed in their pickling juice indefinitely.

Yield: about 2 cups

Braised Leeks

Leeks, a member of the lily family, have a mild and sophisticated flavor. They are delicate enough to serve with fish and light meats without being overwhelming, yet they have just the right amount of bite. They are also excellent with game birds. Braising them increases their mellowness and gives them a tender yet firm texture.

For this recipe, choose leeks that have at least 4 inches of white. Avoid leeks that are overgrown and have a dense, woody middle.

4 medium leeks	5 whole black peppercorns
1½ cups chicken stock	1 bay leaf
½ cup white wine	1 sprig fresh thyme
½ teaspoon salt	

Cut off the green tops of the leeks and reserve them for another use. Trim off the root end of the leeks, leaving just a little bit of the root on the end to hold the leek together. Cut the leek in half lengthwise. Rinse the leek under cold running water, carefully separating the layers to clean out the dirt lurking there.

In a 10-inch nonreactive sauté pan, combine the stock, wine, salt, peppercorns, bay leaf, and thyme. Add the rinsed leeks to the liquid.

Place the pan over medium heat and bring the liquid to a boil. Lower the heat to a gentle simmer and cover the pan. Braise the leeks until they are tender when pierced with a knife tip, about 15 to 20 minutes. Drain before serving.

Yield: 4 servings

NOTE: You can prepare braised leeks a day ahead and refrigerate them in their cooking liquid. Reheat them in the liquid over moderate heat. Reserve the braising liquid for use in soups, stews, or sauces.

Baked Stuffed Onions

This side is for onion lovers only. It can be an elegant side dish for a nice beef entrée, such as a roast prime rib. For companion sides, think of Creamed Spinach (page 129) or Swiss Chard Gratin (page 47) and maybe Rosemary-Scented Roasted Carrots, Turnips, and Shallots (page 23), but leave out the shallots.

When selecting onions for this recipe, choose those that are not too large and that are somewhat flat.

2 strips bacon	Salt and freshly ground pepper
2 tablespoons currants	to taste
1½ cups fresh bread crumbs	Unsalted butter, softened
1 teaspoon curry powder	4 medium onions
Squeeze of fresh lemon juice	

Preheat the oven to 375°F.

Fry the bacon strips until crisp. Drain and crumble the bacon and reserve the fat.

Place the crumbled bacon, currants, bread crumbs, curry powder, lemon juice, salt, and pepper in a bowl. Drizzle in a teaspoon of the reserved bacon fat. Add enough soft butter to moisten the mixture, and combine well.

Peel the onions and trim the root end. With a sharp paring knife, carve a deep hollow into the top of each onion, leaving a layer or two around the edge. Fill with stuffing.

Place the stuffed onions into a baking pan just large enough to hold them without crowding and pour a cup of water around them. Cover with foil and bake until the onions are tender when pierced with a knife—at least 1 hour. Remove the foil during the last few minutes of baking to let the filling brown.

Yield: 4 servings

Spicy Gingered Carrots

These carrots have an irresistible, assertive flavor. They would be best with a simple entrée, like pork chops or chicken. You can slice the carrots into ½-inch pieces or try "roll-cutting" them. To roll-cut, make your first cut on a 45° angle, give the carrot a quarter turn, slice again on the same angle, and so on, up to the top. This gives you an attractive cut, somewhat out of the ordinary.

1¾ cups ½-inch-thick sliced carrots	2 teaspoons unsalted butter
¾ cup chicken stock	¼ teaspoon hot red pepper flakes
4 ¼-inch slices fresh ginger	1 tablespoon honey
	½ teaspoon minced garlic

Combine the carrots, chicken stock, ginger, butter, red pepper flakes, honey, and garlic in a small saucepan. Bring to a boil, then lower the heat and continue cooking the carrots at a low boil, uncovered. Cook for about 15 minutes or until the carrots are soft and nicely glazed. Serve hot.

Yield: 2 servings

Brussels Sprouts with Brown Butter and Pecans

This is a good wintertime dish, a favorite for Thanksgiving. Try it with a gratin or baked squash.

1 pint brussels sprouts	Juice of ½ lemon
2 tablespoons unsalted butter	Salt and freshly ground pepper to taste
½ cup roughly chopped pecans	

Bring 2 quarts of salted water to a boil. Trim the brussels sprouts by cutting off the dry stem and removing any unattractive outer leaves. Cut an *X* into the stem end with the tip of a knife. Boil the sprouts for 5 to 10 minutes, depending on their size, until cooked through. Drain.

Cut each sprout in half. Heat a 10-inch sauté pan over high heat. Add the butter. When it just starts to brown, add the sprouts, pecans, lemon juice, salt, and pepper. Toss rapidly until heated through and serve at once.

Yield: 4 servings

Rosemary-Scented Roasted Carrots, Turnips, and Shallots

Roasting enhances a vegetable's sweetness and earthiness. This side dish is simple to throw together, doesn't require much fuss, and is especially practical when you have the oven fired up for something else. For that reason alone I love this dish with roast leg of lamb, chicken, pork loin, or beef, sometimes tossing the vegetables in with the meat to mingle with its fat and juices. It is essential to use fresh rosemary—evil shards of dried rosemary just won't do. The rosemary is added toward the end of cooking so that it doesn't lose its aromaticity.

When serving a roast and vegetables like these, I prefer to pair them with something creamy, such as a gratin or Creamed Spinach (page 129).

1 tablespoon olive oil or fat from the roasting pan	Salt and freshly ground pepper to taste
2 carrots	1 teaspoon chopped fresh rosemary
3 medium turnips	
1 dozen small shallots or mixed pearl onions	

Preheat the oven to 375° F.

Place the olive oil or fat in an 8-inch sauté pan or a small roasting pan and put the pan in the oven to preheat.

Peel the carrots, turnips, and shallots or onions. Cut the carrots and turnips into pieces roughly 1 inch thick. If the shallots or onions are nice and tiny, leave them whole—otherwise cut them in half.

Add the vegetables to the hot sauté pan. Season with salt and pepper and roast for about 45 minutes, stirring occasionally. Stir in the rosemary and continue roasting for another 10 minutes, until everything is nicely browned and cooked through.

Yield: 2 servings

Braised Baby Bok Choy

If a vegetable can be called adorable, baby bok choy is just that. A younger version of the more commonly seen larger bok choy, baby bok choy is about 6 inches tall with dark green leaves on white stems. It often has small, pretty yellow flowers. Bok choy is in the cabbage family and is widely eaten in China. It is light tasting with pleasantly crisp stems. It is often stir-fried but is also frequently braised.

Serve Braised Baby Bok Choy with Chinese meals. It is also good with simple roast chicken or sautéed chicken cutlet or beef. It is mild enough to complement delicate fish as well. It can be spread out a bit after cooking, for an attractive presentation.

4 heads baby bok choy	**½ teaspoon salt**
1 garlic clove, peeled and crushed	**2 cups chicken stock**
2 ¼-inch-thick slices fresh ginger	

Trim the dry stem ends of the bok choy, but be sure to leave enough stem to keep the head intact.

Place the bok choy in a 12-inch sauté pan. Add the crushed garlic clove, ginger slices, and salt, then pour in the stock.

Place the sauté pan over high heat and bring to a boil. Lower the heat and simmer the bok choy until tender, about 10 minutes. Turn the bok choy over once to ensure even cooking. Test for doneness with the tip of a knife—if the bok choy is tender but still somewhat crisp, it's done.

Remove the bok choy from the pan and serve immediately.

Yield: 4 servings

VARIATION

If you like, you can remove the baby bok choy and keep it warm while you make a little sauce for it from the braising liquid. You have to use some judgment here—it is hard to say exactly how much braising liquid you will have left. If it has reduced and tastes salty, just add some water to give you at least 1½ cups. Bring the liquid to a boil. Reduce it to a simmer, remove the garlic and ginger, and stir in 1 tablespoon cornstarch dissolved in 2 tablespoons of cold water. Stir the sauce a few moments until thickened, taste for seasoning, and pour over the bok choy.

Glazed Endive

This dish serves more as an accent or foil for an entrée than as a substantial side dish. The combination of the light sweet glaze and bitter endive is perfect next to confit, ham, or game.

1 large Belgian endive	**½ teaspoon sugar**
2 teaspoons unsalted butter	**Salt to taste**

Cut the endive lengthwise into quarters. Trim off the core and then cut each quarter into 2 or 3 lengthwise pieces, about ¼ inch wide.

Heat a 10-inch skillet over high heat until very hot. Add the butter and when it's melted, toss in the endive. Sprinkle it with the sugar and salt and sauté rapidly, tossing, until the endive starts to brown and is wilted but still crunchy—1 or 2 minutes. Serve immediately.

Yield: 2 small servings

Sautéed Escarole with Garlic and Lemon

This is a straightforward side dish, often served with pasta or Italian dishes. The firmness of the escarole makes it ideal for sautéing, and its slight bitterness cuts through seemingly rich dishes.

For a second side, try Saffron Pilaf with Almonds and Raisins (page 114) or Potato Tots (page 142).

4 teaspoons olive oil	**Juice of ½ lemon**
1 head escarole, separated into	**Salt and freshly ground pepper**
whole leaves, washed and dried	**to taste**
1 teaspoon minced garlic	

Heat the oil over high heat in a 10-inch sauté pan. Sauté the escarole, tossing, for 1 minute.

Add the garlic and sauté, tossing, for another 2 minutes, at which point the escarole should be wilted. Add the lemon juice, salt, and pepper and serve immediately.

Yield: 2 servings

Braised Endive

Endive is often overlooked as an ingredient for anything other than salad. Cooked, it makes an unusual and somewhat refined side dish. This simple preparation is a perfect accompaniment to all sorts of game, as the bitter leaf offers a foil for the sweet and sometimes rich-seeming meat. Serve it also with assertive fish like tuna, or with steak and roast chicken.

Consider a second side that will not compound the bitterness of the endive, will add texture, and will brighten up the plate a bit. Spicy Gingered Carrots (page 22), Rosemary-Scented Roasted Carrots, Turnips, and Shallots (page 23), or Baked Acorn Squash (page 17), are all good candidates. Apple Fritters (page 60) have a particular affinity for endive.

2 whole large Belgian endives	**2 bay leaves**
1 teaspoon unsalted butter	**1 sprig fresh thyme**
1 to 1½ cups chicken stock	**Salt to taste**
Juice of ½ lemon	**5 whole black peppercorns**

Trim the very end of each endive, being careful not to cut so much that the leaves fall off. Peel off and discard any ugly outside leaves. Cut each endive in half lengthwise.

Heat a 10-inch sauté pan over medium heat. Add the butter and when the foam subsides, place the endives in the pan, cut side down. Sauté the endives, shaking the pan a bit, for 1 to 2 minutes or until the endives have taken on some color.

Turn the endives over and add the chicken stock, lemon juice, bay leaves, thyme, salt, and peppercorns. Raise the heat and bring to a boil. Lower the heat, cover the pan, and simmer gently until the endives are cooked through, about 10 minutes. The endives are done when a toothpick inserted into the thick end goes in easily.

Remove the endives from the broth and make sure no peppercorns are lurking in the leaves. Serve immediately, fanning the leaves out on the plate.

Yield: 2 to 4 servings

NOTE: The endive can be cooked ahead and reheated in its braising liquid.

Chinese-Style Glazed Watercress

This is a quick dish to make, the simple glaze heightening the green taste of the cress. You need only trim a half inch or so off the stems of the watercress, as they will be tender after cooking. Serve this dish with plain meats or fish or a rice or noodle dish.

½ cup chicken stock

½ scallion, cut into 2 or 3 large
    pieces

1 garlic clove, cut in half

2 thin slices fresh ginger

2 teaspoons vegetable oil

1 bunch watercress, washed and
    dried

Salt to taste

1 teaspoon cornstarch, dissolved in
    about 1 tablespoon cold water

Combine the stock, scallion, garlic, and ginger in a small saucepan. Bring to a boil and then reduce the heat and simmer very gently for 15 minutes. Strain, reserving the liquid and discarding the solids.

Heat the vegetable oil in a 10-inch sauté pan over high heat. Add the cress, sprinkle with a little salt, and sauté rapidly, tossing, until it is somewhat wilted, about 2 minutes.

Add the reserved seasoned stock, toss, and bring to a boil. Add the cornstarch mixture and toss until just thickened. Serve immediately.

Yield: 2 servings

Vegetable Quinoa

Quinoa is a very small whole grain with a distinctive nutty flavor. From the Andes in Peru, it is reportedly very high in protein and other nutrients. It makes a filling and healthful side dish, much like bulgur or barley. This particular dish can be served hot the first day and eaten cold as leftovers the next. Its earthy taste complements game particularly well, but serve it with any entrée when a simple, wholesome side is desired. The vegetables should be diced very finely so that they cook sufficiently when tossed with the hot grain. For a second side dish, Winter Vegetable Purée with Sweet Spices and Crispy Shallots (page 40) or Swiss Chard Gratin (page 47) would do nicely.

1 cup quinoa	¾ teaspoon minced garlic
1¼ cups water	Juice of ½ lemon
⅓ cup finely diced zucchini	Salt and freshly ground pepper
⅓ cup finely diced carrots	to taste
⅓ cup finely diced radish	

In a small saucepan, combine the quinoa and water. Bring to a boil over high heat, then reduce to a simmer, cover, and cook for about 15 minutes or until the grain is tender. Remove the lid, fluff the quinoa, and let it stand until the grain dries slightly.

Combine the cooked quinoa with the zucchini, carrot, radish, garlic, lemon juice, salt, and pepper. Toss and serve.

Yield: 4 servings

Fried Rice with Spring Vegetables

This is, of course, a perfect way to use leftover rice. It is healthful and subtle and will enhance almost anything. Have it with delicate fish or shrimp, steamed chicken, or sautéed pork chops. Serve Chinese-Style Dry-Fried Green Beans (page 62) or Spicy Seaweed Salad (page 152) alongside.

4 teaspoons vegetable oil	½ cup shelled fresh peas or thawed
5 ¼-inch-thick slices fresh ginger	frozen peas
1 garlic clove, minced	4 cups cold cooked rice
1 cup sliced asparagus, cut into	2 tablespoons soy sauce
¾-inch pieces (about ¼ pound)	Salt to taste
2 ounces snow peas, cut into	
½-inch pieces	

Heat a 10-inch skillet over high heat until very hot. Add 2 teaspoons of the oil, the ginger, and garlic. Quickly stir-fry until the ginger and garlic are aromatic, but not brown, about 15 seconds.

Quickly add the asparagus and stir-fry for about 30 seconds, until the asparagus starts to turn bright green. Add the snow peas and peas and stir-fry another 20 to 30 seconds, until the vegetables are just barely cooked through and still crunchy. Remove them from the pan to a bowl. Discard the ginger slices.

Let the pan get very hot again and add the remaining 2 teaspoons of oil. Add the rice and stir-fry until it is heated through and slightly browned, about 30 to 45 seconds. Add the soy sauce, return the vegetables to the pan, and stir everything together. Quickly taste for salt, season, and serve immediately.

Yield: 2 to 4 servings

Baked Potato Stuffed with Cabbage and Mushrooms

Stuffed baked potatoes have become quite popular in recent years, but are usually blanketed in sour cream or cheese sauce. While I would never dream of denouncing either, the baked potato recipe here at hand lets the potato flavor come through. The rustic earthiness of both the cabbage and mushrooms enhance that flavor even further.

This would be a perfect accompaniment to beef, and there is not much in the recipe to clash with any meat or firm-fleshed fish.

2 Idaho potatoes	1 cup chopped savoy cabbage, cut
2 teaspoons unsalted butter	into $\frac{1}{2}$-inch dice
4 large cultivated mushrooms	Salt and freshly ground pepper to
1 shallot, chopped	taste

Preheat the oven to 400° F.

Wash the potatoes and prick them several times with a fork. Place them on the oven rack and bake for 1 hour, until a toothpick can easily be inserted into the center.

While the potatoes are baking, melt the butter in an 8-inch sauté pan over high heat. Add the mushrooms and sauté, stirring frequently, until the mushrooms are browned, about 5 minutes.

Lower the heat to medium and add the shallot and cabbage. Continue sautéing until the cabbage is wilted, about another 5 minutes. Reserve until the potatoes are ready. (This may be reheated in the pan when ready to serve.)

When the potatoes are done and just cool enough to handle, cut them in half lengthwise. With a paring knife, carve out the centers, leaving the potato flesh in intact pieces. Cut the pieces into a rough $\frac{1}{2}$-inch size. Combine the potato pieces with the mushroom and cabbage mixture and season with salt and pepper.

Lightly season the potato halves with salt and pepper and fill them with the mushroom mixture. Serve immediately.

Yield: 4 servings

Potato Ragout with Red Wine and Wild Mushrooms

This hearty ragout is great for wintertime meals, alongside a crisply roasted chicken, a pork roast, or a steak. Serve it with a simple green vegetable, such as asparagus or sugar snap peas. You can substitute cultivated white mushrooms for the wild mushrooms if you like.

3 tablespoons olive oil	2 bay leaves
1 small onion, cut in half and sliced lengthwise	$\frac{1}{2}$ pound firm wild mushrooms, such as chanterelles, cremini, or shiitake
12 garlic cloves, peeled	
4 large boiling potatoes, peeled and cut into $\frac{1}{2}$-inch cubes	Salt and freshly ground pepper to taste
$\frac{1}{2}$ cup hearty red wine	2 tablespoons coarsely chopped fresh parsley
2 cups chicken stock	
$\frac{1}{2}$ teaspoon dried thyme	

In a 12-inch skillet, heat 1 tablespoon of the olive oil over medium heat. Add the onion and garlic cloves and sauté about 5 minutes or until the onions are slightly browned.

Add the potatoes and the wine. Raise the heat to high and cook until the wine is reduced by half, about 5 minutes.

Add the stock, thyme, and bay leaves. Bring to a boil, then lower the heat to a simmer and cook for 25 minutes, stirring occasionally.

While the ragout is simmering, trim the tough parts of the mushroom stems and clean any dirt from the mushrooms with a damp cloth. Cut them into large pieces.

In a 10-inch skillet, heat the remaining 2 tablespoons of olive oil over medium heat. Add the mushrooms and cook, stirring occasionally, for about 15 minutes, until they have softened and their juice has evaporated.

Add the mushrooms to the potato ragout and simmer together for about 20 minutes.

Season the ragout with salt and pepper. Just before serving, remove the bay leaf and stir in the parsley.

Yield: 6 servings

NOTE: The ragout reheats well, but you may need to add a little stock or water.

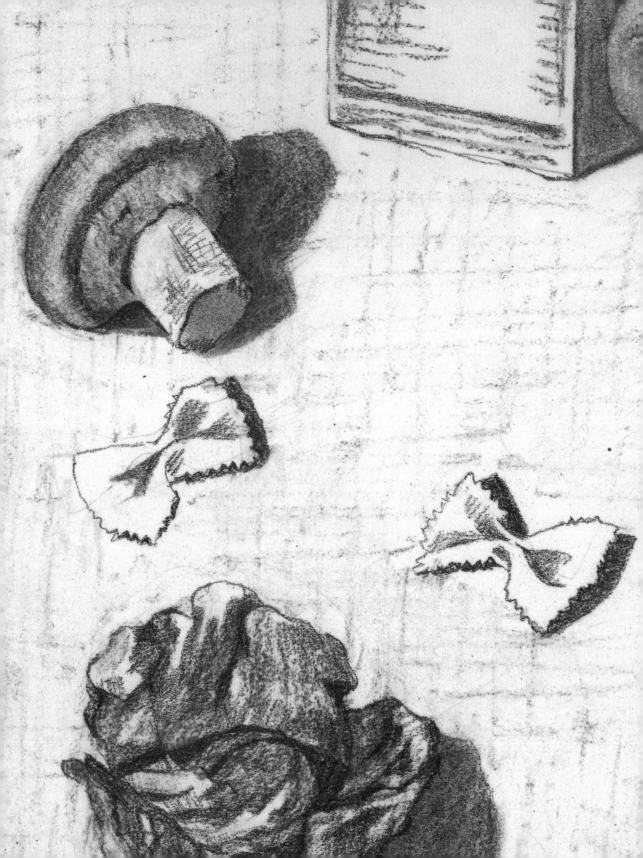

Gratins, Purées, and Other Soothing Sides

I will never get tired of gratins—never. To me they are the ultimate sides. These sides are delightful for the way they cohabit with main courses. They do not sit idly by, observing the piece of meat or fish from a distance. Rather, they interact and get involved, happy to have someone to play with. When I plan a menu, I often start knowing I want to make a turnip or potato gratin, for example, and then build the rest of my meal around it. Once you become familiar with the basic methods for making gratins, you can use your imagination to create flavor combinations that suit your own tastes.

Gratins, purées, and molded custards are also good vehicles for embellishing inexpensive ingredients using a simple technique. Carrots are an everyday vegetable, but made into a purée with a little orange zest, or turned into a custard, they become exceptional. These types of sides are flexible in their style as well, being equally at home with a rustic or an elegant meal. And because purées can be made ahead of time and gently reheated several times over without damage, they are especially useful dishes for entertaining.

Potato Gratin with Onion and Thyme ◆ *Potato Gratin with Herbs and Chicken Essence* ◆ *Potato Gratin with Ham and Nutmeg* ◆ *Mashed Potato Casserole* ◆ *Turnip Gratin* ◆ *Winter Vegetable Purée with Sweet Spices and Crispy Shallots* ◆ *Parsnip Purée with Orange* ◆ *Turnip Purée with Garlic Butter* ◆ *Carrot Purée with Almonds* ◆ *White Bean Purée* ◆ *Spinach-Wrapped Zucchini Flan* ◆ *Gratinéed Braised Fennel* ◆ *Swiss Chard Gratin* ◆ *Corn Custard* ◆ *Carrot Custard Pie* ◆ *Macaroni and Cheese* ◆ *Bow-Tie Gratin with Radicchio and Mushrooms* ◆ *Egg Noodle Gratin* ◆ *Potato and Goat Cheese Terrine*

Potato Gratin with Onion and Thyme

A potato gratin is one of those rich and creamy dishes that is irresistible, yet simple to prepare. Served alongside a perfectly roasted beef or chicken, or a stew redolent of wine or mushrooms, a potato gratin brings a meal all together. There are many variations on this theme—some cooks blanch the potatoes before adding cream, milk, or whatever, but I find this unnecessary if the potatoes are soaked or at least rinsed in water before baking to remove some of the starch. You can certainly vary the recipe by adding other ingredients—sautéed mushrooms, cheese, ham (as on page 38)—use your imagination. The idea here is to learn the technique. And don't worry about the cream unless you have health problems; you cannot go through life avoiding such wonderful gustatory pleasures, or the stress will kill you.

2 large Idaho potatoes

Salt and freshly ground pepper to
  taste

1 small onion, peeled and sliced

1 teaspoon chopped fresh thyme

1 pint heavy cream

A couple pats of butter

Peel the potatoes (or not, as you wish), slice them thinly, and soak them in cold water for at least 1 hour or even overnight in the refrigerator. If you are in a rush, at least rinse the potato slices very well in cold running water. Drain the slices and spread them out on a kitchen towel. Pat them fairly dry with the towel and then liberally salt and pepper them. (Don't forget that potatoes need a lot of salt.)

Preheat the oven to 350° F.

Grease a 6-cup gratin dish with butter. Place half the potato slices in the dish in an even layer. Layer in all the onion slices, sprinkle with the chopped thyme, and then top with the rest of the potato. Pour the cream over the top. Dot with the butter and bake for 40 minutes, until the gratin is cooked through and brown and bubbly on top. Serve immediately.

Yield: 4 servings

Potato Gratin with Herbs and Chicken Essence

This gratin, made with chicken stock instead of cream, is wonderfully full flavored. It is suitable for serving with a casual dinner as well as a more formal one. Its mellow, unaggressive flavor makes it quite versatile when pairing with an entrée or other side dishes. Leftovers are great panfried in a nonstick skillet.

3 medium Idaho potatoes	Salt and freshly ground pepper to taste
1 small onion, peeled and sliced	
2 tablespoons chopped mixed fresh herbs, such as chives, tarragon, parsley, oregano, chervil, thyme, or some combination thereof	2 cups chicken stock

Preheat the oven to 375° F.

Peel and thinly slice the potatoes. Rinse the slices well under cold running water and drain well.

Layer a third of the potatoes in the bottom of a greased 6-cup gratin dish. Layer in half the sliced onion and sprinkle with half the herbs. Season with salt and pepper.

Add another layer of half the remaining potatoes and the rest of the onions and herbs. Season again with salt and pepper and then top with a third layer of potatoes. Season a final time with salt and pepper.

Pour the chicken stock over the gratin and bake about 50 minutes or until tender when tested with a knife. Serve immediately.

Yield: 4 to 6 servings

Potato Gratin with Ham and Nutmeg

Yet another potato gratin, this one has a smoky essence derived from the ham. Serve it with something that might benefit from the ham flavor, like roast chicken with a light white wine sauce, perhaps, or a shellfish dish; shrimp, lobster, clams, and oysters all have an affinity for ham.

Since the gratin is creamy, choose another side dish to provide balance. Something with a bit of astringency, like spinach or tomatoes, would work.

2 large Idaho potatoes	Salt and freshly ground pepper
Scant ½ cup chopped ham, such as	to taste
Canadian bacon	1 cup heavy cream
A few gratings of nutmeg	1 tablespoon unsalted butter, cut
	into bits

Peel the potatoes (or don't, as you wish), slice them thinly, and soak them in cold water for at least 1 hour or even overnight in the refrigerator. If you are in a rush, at least rinse the potato slices very well under cold running water. Drain the slices and spread them out on a kitchen towel. Pat them fairly dry with the towel.

Preheat the oven to 375° F.

Grease a 6-cup gratin dish with butter. Layer in a third of the potato slices. Sprinkle with half the chopped ham and sprinkle lightly with nutmeg. Season with salt and pepper (don't forget that potatoes need a lot of salt). Make another layer with half the remaining potatoes, sprinkle on the remaining ham, and lightly dust again with nutmeg. Season again with salt and pepper. Top with the remaining potatoes and season a final time with salt and pepper.

Pour the cream over the gratin and dot with the butter. Bake for 40 minutes or until the gratin is browned and bubbly. Serve immediately.

Yield: 2 to 4 servings

Mashed Potato Casserole

This casserole can be prepared a day ahead and put into the oven 45 to 60 minutes before you are ready to serve it. It's perfect for party buffets, as it retains heat fairly well or can be kept on a warmer without damage. Of course, you may not need to worry about keeping it hot—it probably won't hang around very long!

The flavors here are versatile, so serve this casserole whenever potatoes seem appropriate. The recipe may seem to contain a lot of garlic, but not to worry. The flavor is actually not very aggressive because the garlic is rendered mild and sweet as it boils with the potatoes. In fact, garlic lovers will want to add even more.

4 pounds Idaho potatoes	**3 tablespoons grated Parmesan**
1 head garlic	**Salt and freshly ground pepper**
1 cup heavy cream	**to taste**
2 tablespoons unsalted butter	**¼ cup dry bread crumbs**
2 eggs	

Peel the potatoes and cut them in half.

Peel the garlic cloves and trim off the hard tips.

Combine the potatoes and garlic in a large pot and cover with cold salted water. Bring to a boil over high heat. Lower the heat and keep the potatoes at a low boil until they are tender, about 30 minutes. Drain.

Preheat the oven to 375° F.

Whip the potatoes and garlic, using an electric beater, along with the cream, butter, eggs, Parmesan, salt, and pepper. Try not to leave any lumps—they are more noticeable in a casserole than in mashed potatoes served the usual way.

Place the mashed potatoes in a 2½-quart casserole and sprinkle the bread crumbs over the top. Bake for 30 to 45 minutes, until the casserole is heated through and somewhat puffy around the edges.

Yield: 6 to 8 servings

Turnip Gratin

I have often served this gratin with duck or steak and been asked why the potatoes were so delicious. People are often stunned to find out they've enjoyed turnips so much!

Serve this with greens, such as Kale with Bacon and Onion (page 127) or sugar snaps.

5 or 6 large turnips	**2 cups heavy cream**
Salt and freshly ground pepper	**1 tablespoon unsalted butter, cut**
to taste	**into 4 bits**

Preheat the oven to 350° F.

Peel the turnips and slice them thinly. Place them in a 6-cup gratin dish and sprinkle with the salt and pepper. Toss to distribute the seasonings thoroughly and then arrange the turnip slices evenly.

Pour the cream over the turnips—it should just cover them. Dot with the butter and bake for 45 to 60 minutes until the turnips are tender, the cream has reduced, and the top of the gratin is browned.

Yield: 4 servings

Winter Vegetable Purée with Sweet Spices and Crispy Shallots

The sweet spices give this purée a holiday feeling, reminiscent of mulled cider or pumpkin pie. A bit of cream or butter may be added for extra richness while puréeing the vegetables, but it is not necessary. Try this with roast turkey, chicken, or pork. Other appropriate side dishes would be winter vegetables like Brussels Sprouts with Brown Butter and Pecans (page 22), Slow-Braised Red Cabbage (page 16), or Sautéed Barley with Duck Fat and Kale (page 130).

1 tablespoon unsalted butter

1 small onion, peeled and diced

2 garlic cloves, peeled and chopped

1 small butternut squash, peeled, seeded, and diced

2 small or 1 large acorn squash, peeled, seeded, and diced

2 large turnips, peeled and diced

2 carrots, peeled and cut into 1-inch-thick rounds

1½ cups chicken stock

½ teaspoon dried thyme

1 bay leaf

½ teaspoon ground cinnamon

⅛ teaspoon grated nutmeg

¼ teaspoon ground ginger

Small pinch of cayenne pepper

Small pinch of allspice

1 teaspoon kosher salt

A few grinds of black pepper

Squeeze of fresh lemon juice

½ cup heavy cream or 2 tablespoons unsalted butter (optional)

FOR THE SHALLOTS

3 large shallots

Vegetable or olive oil, for frying

Salt to taste

In a 3-quart saucepan, melt the butter over medium heat. Add the onion and garlic and sweat them until translucent, but not browned, about 5 minutes.

Add the butternut and acorn squash, turnips, and carrots. Cover and sweat for 5 minutes, stirring occasionally.

Add the stock and the thyme, bay leaf, cinnamon, nutmeg, ginger, cayenne, allspice, kosher salt, and pepper. Bring to a boil over high heat, then lower the heat to a simmer and cook for about 30 minutes, until the vegetables are soft. Stir occasionally.

While the vegetables are cooking, prepare the shallots. Trim off both ends, cut them in half lengthwise, and then thinly slice them lengthwise. You should get half-moon pieces. Heat ¼ inch of oil in a 10-inch frying pan over medium heat. Fry the shallots in 2 batches until golden brown (the shallot should sizzle on contact with the oil), about 30 seconds. Drain on paper towels and salt lightly. The shallots will get crispier when they cool and may be made a day ahead—just cover them well and keep them at room temperature.

Purée the vegetables in a food processor or blender, adding a little cream or butter if desired. Season with a squeeze of lemon juice and then taste and adjust the seasonings. Serve the purée in a shallow bowl and sprinkle the crispy shallots on top.

Yield: 4 to 6 servings

Parsnip Purée with Orange

Like the other purées in this book, this one can swing both ways—casual or formal. I think this dish goes particularly well with pork. A leafy green, like escarole, or string beans would be a good second.

4 cups sliced parsnips, cut about ½ inch thick	¼ teaspoon grated orange zest
2-inch strip orange zest	1 tablespoon unsalted butter, cut into bits
1 cup chicken stock	Salt and freshly ground pepper
Juice of 1 orange	to taste

Combine the parsnips, orange zest, and stock in a 10-inch skillet. Bring to a boil over high heat, lower the heat to a simmer, and cover the pan. Cook for about half an hour, until the parsnips are soft. Discard the orange zest.

Pass the parsnips and what is left of the cooking liquid through a food mill or purée them in a food processor. Stir in the orange juice, grated zest, butter, salt, and pepper and serve immediately.

Yield: 4 servings

N O T E : This can be made a few days ahead. You can either reheat it gently on top of the stove, stirring often, or put the purée in an ovenproof casserole and reheat, covered, in a 375° F. oven. You can also leave the casserole uncovered and top it with buttered crumbs if you like.

Turnip Purée with Garlic Butter

This purée can be served with just about any meat; it is at home at both casual and more formal meals. A leafy green like spinach would complement it nicely.

6 large turnips (1½ to 2 pounds)	3 tablespoons unsalted butter
1 Idaho potato	Salt and freshly ground pepper to taste
2 garlic cloves, peeled	taste
½ cup heavy cream	1 teaspoon minced garlic

Peel the turnips and potato and cut them into large chunks. Place them in a 3-quart saucepan with the whole garlic cloves and cover with salted water. Bring to a boil over high heat, reduce the heat, and continue cooking at a low boil until the vegetables are tender, about 45 to 55 minutes.

Drain the vegetables and pass them through a food mill or whip them with an electric beater until smooth. Stir in the cream, 1 tablespoon of the butter, salt, and pepper. Transfer the purée to a casserole serving dish without smoothing the top—leave it wavy.

Melt the remaining 2 tablespoons of butter in a small skillet over medium heat. Add the teaspoon of minced garlic and sauté it until it just barely begins to color, about 30 seconds. Pour the garlic butter over the turnip purée and serve immediately.

Yield: 4 to 6 servings

Carrot Purée with Almonds

This is another elegant, somewhat feminine dish but one that is suitable for a wide range of entrées. It is delicious with darker meats like lamb or duck.

4 medium carrots	**A grating of nutmeg**
1 tablespoon unsalted butter, cut into bits	**Salt and freshly ground pepper to taste**
1 tablespoon heavy cream	**1 tablespoon toasted almonds**

Peel the carrots, trim the ends, and cut them into 2-inch lengths. Boil them in salted water until thoroughly cooked, 35 to 40 minutes depending on the size and age of the carrots.

Drain the carrots well. Place them in a food processor or blender with the butter, cream, nutmeg, and salt and pepper, and purée. You can use your judgment here to make a coarser or finer purée, depending on your preference.

There are several possibilities for serving. You can garnish the plate directly, sprinkling the carrot purée with the toasted almonds, or serve it in a shallow bowl, using a butter knife to make "waves" on the surface, and then garnish with the almonds. You can also pipe the purée from a pastry bag onto plates, and then sprinkle it with the almonds.

Yield: 2 servings

White Bean Purée

This is a robust, gutsy side dish that is delicious with lamb. I would also serve it with firm-fleshed seafood like tuna or shrimp, as well as with any meat. Its heartiness does not prevent it from being neutral enough to accommodate many entrée flavors and preparations.

For a second side, choose something with a contrasting texture, like Rosemary-Scented Roasted Carrots, Turnips, and Shallots (page 23) or Sautéed Escarole with Garlic and Lemon (page 25).

White Bean Purée is also a great spread or dip to serve with pita wedges, crackers, or crudités.

1 pound dried white beans, such as Great Northern	1 cup chicken stock
1 tablespoon olive oil	Salt and freshly ground pepper to taste
2 teaspoons minced garlic	A grating of nutmeg
1 medium onion, peeled and diced	Pinch of cayenne pepper
1 carrot, peeled and diced	

In a large saucepan, cover the beans with 10 cups of cold water and bring to a boil over high heat. Lower the heat and then simmer the beans for approximately 1½ hours, stirring occasionally, until tender.

In a 12-inch sauté pan, heat the olive oil over medium-low heat. Add the garlic, onion, and carrot and sauté, stirring occasionally, for 5 minutes. Be careful not to let the vegetables brown.

Add the cooked beans, chicken stock, and seasonings to the pan and simmer gently, stirring occasionally, for 5 to 10 minutes, until the vegetables are soft and the beans are hot.

Place the bean mixture in the bowl of a food processor and purée it. You may have to do this in 2 batches. Transfer the purée to a bowl, taste it, and adjust the seasonings. Serve the bean purée in a bowl or a casserole, or on a platter.

Yield: 8 servings

NOTE: White Bean Purée keeps well in the refrigerator for 2 or 3 days. Reheat either in a sauté pan on top of the stove over a gentle heat with a little stock or water or place the purée in a casserole, top with buttered bread crumbs if desired, and place in a 350° F. oven for at least 30 minutes.

Spinach~Wrapped Zucchini Flan

Flans are good dinner-party side dishes because you can make them a day ahead and pop them in the oven at the last minute to reheat—and they add a bit of elegance. Pair them with another side dish that adds textural and color contrast and stay away from mashed or creamed sides. Sautéed Mushrooms with Oregano (page 8) comes to mind.

Serve these flans with any roast or sauté, whether it be lamb chops, chicken scallopini, or roast beef. They are also delicate enough to complement fish like sole or snapper and shrimp.

1 large zucchini (about ¾ pound)	**A few gratings of nutmeg**
½ cup heavy cream	**Tiny pinch of curry powder**
2 eggs	**Tiny pinch of cayenne pepper**
1 egg yolk	**4 to 6 large leaves flat-leafed**
Salt and freshly ground pepper	**spinach**
to taste	

Preheat the oven to 300° F.

Trim the ends of the zucchini and cut it into 2-inch chunks. Steam the zucchini for about 20 minutes, until it is cooked through and soft. When it is cool enough to handle, squeeze the zucchini to get out as much liquid as possible. Transfer to the bowl of a food processor.

Process the zucchini for 30 seconds. Add the cream, eggs, egg yolk, salt, pepper, nutmeg, curry powder, and cayenne and process until very smooth.

While the zucchini is steaming, gently pull the stems off the spinach and wash the leaves. Put them in the steamer for a minute or two, until they are just wilted. Remove the spinach leaves and spread them out flat on paper towels. Pat them very dry.

Grease four 4-ounce ramekins thoroughly with unsalted butter. Use the spinach to line each ramekin, positioning the leaves with the ribbed side inward. Try to make sure that there are no tears on the bottom. Leave a little spinach overhanging the edges of the ramekins.

Gently fill the ramekins with the zucchini custard. Fold the spinach over the custard.

Place the ramekins in a roasting or cake pan. Fill the pan with tepid water ⅔ of the way up the sides of the ramekins. Bake for about 45 minutes or until the custard is just set. Be careful not to let the flans puff or cook too fast, or they will curdle. Remove the ramekins from the water bath and let them rest 5 minutes before unmolding onto dinner plates.

Yield: 4 servings

Gratinéed Braised Fennel

Fennel has an assertive character that must be taken into consideration when pairing it with other dishes. It is often used in Italian-style preparations and has an affinity for flavors such as garlic, tomato, oregano, and Parmesan. Serve this gratinéed version with baked pasta dishes, tomato-based stews like cacciatore, or with something simpler, such as a pork roast. The wispy fennel tops make great plate garnishes.

1 large fennel bulb	¼ cup dry bread crumbs
1 cup chicken stock	½ teaspoon dried thyme
½ teaspoon salt	½ teaspoon dried oregano
A few grinds of black pepper	1 tablespoon olive oil
2 bay leaves	

Preheat the oven to 375° F.

Cut off the top of the fennel bulb, reserving some of the sprigs. Trim the base of the bulb and remove any unattractive outer layers. Chop about 1 teaspoon of the fennel sprigs, set them aside, and reserve the rest for plate garnishes if desired.

Cut the bulb in half the long way and place cut side down in a shallow ovenproof dish, such as a pie pan or gratin dish. Pour the chicken stock over the fennel, sprinkle with ¼ teaspoon salt (if using canned stock that has salt added, omit the salt here) and the pepper, add the bay leaves, and loosely cover the dish with foil. Bake for 40 minutes.

Uncover the fennel and continue cooking, letting the chicken stock reduce, until the fennel is tender when pierced with a fork or skewer, about another 20 minutes, depending on the size of the bulb. The stock should become saucelike, but if it looks like it might evaporate before the fennel is done, add a little water.

While the fennel is baking, prepare the topping by combining the chopped fennel tops, bread crumbs, thyme, oregano, remaining ¼ teaspoon salt, a few grinds of pepper, and the olive oil in a small bowl. Stir until well blended.

When the fennel is tender, remove it from the oven. Sprinkle with the topping and return it to the oven for 5 minutes. Just before serving, place under the broiler to brown.

Yield: 2 servings

NOTE: This may be reheated in a 375° F. oven for about 20 minutes.

Swiss Chard Gratin

If you love greens, you will find this dish irresistible. It is especially good with roasts, but also with shrimp. Serve it with Potato Cake with Scallion (page 70), Spaetzle (page 139), or plain rice.

1 large bunch white Swiss chard

1 garlic clove

Salt and freshly ground pepper to
   taste

1 cup heavy cream

2 tablespoons grated Parmesan

Preheat the oven to 450° F.

Trim the ends of the Swiss chard but leave on the stems. Wash it well. Using only the water clinging to the leaves, steam the chard in a large pot until it is just wilted, about 5 minutes. Drain the Swiss chard and roughly chop it. You should have about 2 cups of cooked chard.

Peel the garlic clove and smash it with the flat side of a knife. Rub the sides and bottom of a 4- or 6-cup gratin dish with the garlic, then discard the garlic.

Place the cooked chard in the gratin dish and season with salt and pepper. Pour the cream over the Swiss chard and sprinkle with the Parmesan.

Bake the gratin until the cream has reduced and thickened and the Parmesan is lightly browned, about 20 minutes. If the cream has thickened but the Parmesan is not brown enough, place the gratin under the broiler for 30 seconds or so. Serve immediately.

Yield: 2 to 4 servings

Corn Custard

This is best made with fresh corn cut off the cob, but I have also prepared it with canned corn with delicious results. The corn flavor infuses the custard with its sweetness and essence.

Serve Corn Custard with chicken or veal but also with fish and seafood. Lobster, shrimp, and oysters all have a special affinity for this dish.

½ cup fresh corn kernels (about 1 ear), coarsely chopped

1 cup heavy cream

2 eggs

1 egg yolk

1 small shallot, minced

½ teaspoon salt

3 grinds of black pepper

Tiny pinch of cayenne pepper

A grating of nutmeg

Preheat the oven to 325°F.

Combine the corn, cream, eggs, egg yolk, shallot, salt, pepper, cayenne, and nutmeg in a mixing bowl and whisk very well to combine thoroughly.

Grease well four 4-ounce ramekins with butter. Ladle the custard mixture into the ramekins, making sure that each one gets a fair amount of corn kernels.

Place the ramekins in a roasting pan or cake pan. Fill the pan with tepid water ⅔ of the way up the sides of the ramekins. Make sure the ramekins are not touching each other.

Bake the custards for about 45 minutes, until they are just set; be careful not to let them puff. If they look like they are cooking too fast, lower the oven temperature by 25°. When they are done, remove the custards from the water bath and let them rest 5 minutes before unmolding.

To unmold, run a thin knife around the edge of each custard. Then either invert the ramekin directly onto a dinner plate or else onto a flat metal spatula from which you can slide it onto a plate.

Yield: 4 servings

NOTE: You can cook the custards a day ahead, let them cool, wrap them in plastic, and refrigerate. To reheat, place them in a 350°F. oven for about 10 minutes, until hot.

Carrot Custard Pie

This is a good example of how you can transform a simple vegetable, such as the carrot, into something special. It's a festive dish, one that can dress up a plain roast or be served with the Thanksgiving turkey (talk about a plain roast!). For a more elegant presentation, make small individual pies.

Just about any other side dish will go with this, but if I was serving only one I'd choose a green like Kale with Bacon and Onion (page 127).

1 recipe Tart Pastry (page 192)	Small pinch of curry powder
1¾ cups sliced carrots	Small pinch of cayenne pepper
¾ cup milk	Small pinch of freshly grated
1 egg	nutmeg
1 egg yolk	Salt and freshly ground pepper
¼ teaspoon minced garlic	to taste

Preheat the oven to 375°F.

Roll out the pie dough to about ⅛ inch thick. Place the pastry in a 9-inch pie pan and weigh it down with pie weights or dried beans. Bake it for 15 to 20 minutes, until the dough is set and about halfway baked. Remove the weights and let the crust cool while you prepare the custard. Lower the temperature of the oven to 350°F.

Cook the carrots in boiling salted water for about 20 minutes, until soft. Drain, and chill under cold running water. Drain well and pat dry.

Place the cooked carrots in the bowl of a food processor. Add the milk, egg, egg yolk, garlic, curry powder, cayenne, nutmeg, salt, and pepper and process until smooth.

Pour the custard into the prebaked pie shell and bake for 30 to 35 minutes, until it is just set in the middle. Let the pie rest a few minutes and serve hot.

Yield: 8 servings

Macaroni and Cheese

Macaroni and cheese is another of those quintessential American side dishes. It's great with all kinds of barbecue, fried chicken and pork chops, roast chicken or beef. Use the sharpest cheddar you can find or its flavor will get lost in the cooking. Serve a green alongside, such as Kale with Bacon and Onion (page 127), Southern Collard Greens (page 128), or just some plain steamed greens.

½ pound elbow uncooked
    macaroni

4 tablespoons (½ stick) unsalted
    butter

3 tablespoons all-purpose flour

1 teaspoon minced garlic

2 cups milk

A few gratings of nutmeg

A few grinds of black pepper

1½ cups grated extra-sharp
    cheddar cheese

Salt to taste

½ teaspoon dry mustard

Squeeze of fresh lemon juice

½ cup dry bread crumbs

Preheat the oven to 400° F.

Drop the elbow macaroni into 3 quarts of boiling salted water and cook, stirring occasionally, for 7 minutes. It should still be underdone at this point. Drain.

In a heavy-bottomed, nonreactive 3-quart saucepan, melt 3 tablespoons of the butter over medium-low heat. Whisk in the flour and continue whisking for 3 minutes or until the roux gives off a faint nutty aroma. Turn the heat down if the mixture starts to brown.

Add the garlic and whisk for 30 seconds or until the garlic becomes fragrant.

Whisk in ½ cup of the milk to form a smooth, thick paste with the roux. Add another ½ cup and whisk until it is also smooth. Add the rest of the milk, whisking until there are no lumps left. Add the nutmeg and black pepper. Bring the sauce to a gentle simmer and cook, stirring often, for 15 minutes.

Add the grated cheddar, salt, and dry mustard and stir until the cheese has melted and is fully incorporated. Add a squeeze of lemon juice, taste, and adjust the seasonings. Check the sauce for thickness—it should be fairly thick, like hollandaise. Thin it with a little milk, if necessary.

Stir in the cooked macaroni. Pour the macaroni and cheese into a greased 6-cup casserole or gratin dish. Sprinkle the bread crumbs evenly over the top and dot with the remaining tablespoon of butter. Cover with foil and bake for 20 minutes. Remove the foil and continue baking for 10 to 15 minutes or until the top has browned nicely and the casserole is bubbling.

Yield: 4 servings

Bow-Tie Gratin with Radicchio and Mushrooms

This recipe was inspired by a wonderful dinner I had at a friend's house, at which she served a perfectly roasted chicken and this gratin. The meal was a prime example of how a well-chosen side dish can make a simple meal memorable.

$1\frac{1}{2}$ **cups uncooked bow-tie pasta**

2 teaspoons olive oil

5 ounces mushrooms (cremini, shiitake, button, etc.), sliced

$\frac{1}{4}$ **pound radicchio, roughly chopped**

$1\frac{1}{2}$ **cups heavy cream**

Salt and freshly ground pepper to taste

$\frac{1}{4}$ **cup grated Parmesan**

Preheat the oven to 400° F.

Cook the pasta in boiling salted water until al dente. Leave the pasta more al dente than you normally might because it will soften considerably during baking. Drain and reserve.

Heat the olive oil in a 10-inch skillet over high heat. Add the mushroom slices and sauté, tossing frequently, until the mushrooms are browned, 2 to 3 minutes.

Combine the cooked pasta, sautéed mushrooms, radicchio, cream, salt, and pepper in a 6-cup gratin dish or shallow casserole. Stir to combine and then sprinkle the Parmesan over the gratin.

Bake the gratin for 25 to 30 minutes, until the cream has thickened and the gratin is browned on top. Serve immediately.

Yield: 4 servings

Egg Noodle Gratin

This is a basic but really good noodle gratin. Serve it with lots of stuff—roast, sautéed, or grilled birds; birds cooked in red wine; steaks; roast beef; beef stew; leg of lamb; lamb chops—I could go on and on. Some simple steamed greens or sautéed string beans would be perfect as an accompaniment.

2 cups uncooked wide egg noodles	**Salt and freshly ground pepper**
1 teaspoon minced garlic	**to taste**
1 tablespoon chopped shallot	**2 cups heavy cream**
	2 tablespoons grated Parmesan

Preheat the oven to 375°F.

Cook the noodles in boiling salted water until al dente, 10 to 15 minutes. Leave them more al dente than you normally might, because they will soften further in the oven.

Combine the noodles, garlic, shallot, salt, pepper, and cream in a greased 6-cup gratin dish and mix together. Sprinkle the Parmesan on top and bake for about 30 minutes, until the gratin is bubbling and browned. Serve immediately.

Yield: 4 servings

Potato and Goat Cheese Terrine

This lovely side dish is appropriate for a more refined meal; rack of lamb, light-fleshed game birds, veal or seafood, such as shrimp or tuna, would be good partners. When considering sauce, think of pairing this terrine with those made from white wine, vinegar, or lemon rather than red wine.

For complementary side dishes, look first of all for a green that will set off the yellow of the curried goat cheese, such as Corn, Red Pepper, and Green Bean Sauté (page 12) or some simple steamed green.

3 large boiling potatoes	**Salt and freshly ground pepper**
¼ cup heavy cream	**to taste**
1 teaspoon mild Madras-style	**Squeeze of fresh lemon juice**
curry powder	
8 ounces mild goat cheese, at room	
temperature	

Preheat the oven to 350°F.

Trim the potatoes, making them into regular rectangles or squares. Carefully pare off what is left of the peel. Cut the potatoes into ¼-inch slices. Blanch the slices in boiling salted water for about 5 minutes or until just done. Be careful not to overcook them, or they will be difficult to handle. Drain and cool the potato slices.

While the potatoes are cooking, combine the cream and curry powder in a small saucepan and bring just to a boil. Pour the cream into a bowl and cool it to room temperature in the refrigerator.

Place the goat cheese in a mixing bowl. When the cream has cooled, add it to the cheese. Mix with an electric mixer until smooth and creamy. Taste and then season with salt, pepper, and lemon juice.

Thoroughly grease a 6-cup terrine with olive oil or line it with parchment paper. Start assembling the terrine by laying slices of potato edge to edge on the bottom of the terrine, not overlapping but covering the entire surface. (The square shape of the slices should make this easy.)

With a spatula, spread a ¼-inch layer of goat cheese mixture over the potatoes, being careful to do this neatly and evenly. Continue building the terrine, alternating layers of potato and cheese, ending with potato. There should be 4 layers of potato and 3 of cheese.

If using parchment, fold it over the top of the terrine. If not, cover the top of the terrine with aluminum foil. Place the terrine in a roasting pan and fill it with tepid water ⅔ of the way up the side of the terrine, and bake for about an hour or until a knife inserted into the center comes out hot. Remove the terrine from the water bath and let it stand for 10 minutes. Carefully invert the terrine onto a serving platter and serve immediately.

Yield: 8 to 10 servings

NOTE: It's best to use a long, sharp slicing knife to cut the terrine.

Fritters and Other Fried Delights

Fritters and other fried foods never fail to make people happy. We love the hot and crispy exteriors and soft steamy insides of fried foods—they are delicious and fun to eat. Children especially love them.

Fritters offer textural contrast at times when something crunchy is needed in the meal. If the main course has a soft texture, or the other sides are purées, for example, a fritter can provide the necessary counterpart to liven up the plate. Fritters also do a lot for the mood of a meal. If your theme is casual, they already fit right in, and their appearance at a more formal meal can deliver just the right amount of whimsy to make sure things don't get too stodgy. And, of course, they are perfect for sopping up the most elegant of sauces.

Many vegetables are conducive to frying. They can be diced, sliced, or left in larger pieces and featured alone or in pleasing combinations. Fritter batter can be thinned for a lighter coating or thickened for an extra crunch. For variation, spices can be added to the batter to complement whatever vegetable you're using.

Fried Tomatoes ◆ *Plantains with Garlic and Butter* ◆ *Apple Fritters* ◆ *Broccoli Tempura* ◆ *Chinese-Style Dry-Fried Green Beans* ◆ *Fried Zucchini with Black and White Sesame Seeds, Japanese Style* ◆ *Grated Zucchini Cake* ◆ *Curried Vidalia Onion Fritters* ◆ *Mashed Black Bean Cakes with Cilantro* ◆ *Hush Puppies* ◆ *Crispy New England Corn Cakes with Scallions* ◆ *Potato Fritters with Cornichons and Bacon* ◆ *Potato Cake with Scallion* ◆ *Curried Potato Chips* ◆ *Baked Potato Chips* ◆ *Barbecue-Flavored French Fries*

Fried Tomatoes

Yes, you can make this with green tomatoes, but I like red ones. Try to use tomatoes that are ripe, but not overly so. You can bread the tomatoes a few hours ahead and refrigerate uncovered until ready to fry if you prefer.

Fried Tomatoes are great with fish or shellfish, as well as beef and chicken. Steamed spinach (page 130), Saffron Pilaf with Almonds and Raisins (page 114)—leave out the almonds and raisins—or Chilled Lentils with Extra Virgin Olive Oil and Parsley (page 158) are good accompaniments. These Fried Tomatoes are also wonderful for breakfast with poached eggs.

2 medium tomatoes	**Dry bread crumbs, for dredging**
All-purpose flour, for dredging	**Salt to taste**
1 egg, beaten	**Olive oil, for frying**

Slice the tomatoes ½ inch thick.

Place the flour in a bowl, the beaten egg in a second bowl, and the bread crumbs and salt in a third bowl.

Dredge a tomato slice in flour. Dip it in the egg, making sure the egg soaks the flour. Drain over the egg bowl and then dredge it in the bread crumbs. Place the breaded tomato on a sheet pan. Continue with the rest of the tomatoes, laying them side by side, but not touching.

In a 10-inch or 12-inch sauté pan, heat ¼ inch of olive oil over medium heat. Test the oil by dropping in a few bread crumbs—they should sizzle on contact. Fry the tomatoes in batches, 3 or 4 at a time, until golden brown, about 1 minute. Turn the tomatoes over and fry until browned on the other side, about another minute. Drain the tomatoes on paper towels and serve immediately.

Yield: 4 servings

NOTE: The fried tomatoes may be kept briefly in a warm oven while you cook the rest.

Plantains with Garlic and Butter

Plantains are available in many supermarkets and local vegetable stores. They are a member of the banana family and are less sweet and more starchy than the ordinary yellow banana. They are eaten both ripe and unripe, usually fried, baked, stewed, or mashed. The unripe plantain has a green skin, which will turn more yellow and develop black spots as it ripens.

When planning a meal, think of plantains as a starch accompaniment, rather than a fruit. They are delicious with pork or chicken. Serve them with rice and a green vegetable.

1 green plantain	**1 tablespoon unsalted butter**
$\frac{1}{4}$ cup vegetable oil, for frying	**1 teaspoon minced garlic**
Salt to taste	

Peel the plantain (you may have to use a knife). Cut it on an angle into $\frac{1}{4}$-inch slices.

Place the vegetable oil in a 10-inch skillet and heat it over medium-high heat. Test the temperature by dipping in the edge of a plantain slice—it should immediately sizzle. Fry the plantain slices in 2 batches, turning them over once and cooking them until a light golden brown—about 1 to 2 minutes. Remove the slices, blot on paper towels, and then arrange them on a serving platter. Sprinkle with salt.

In a small saucepan or skillet, melt the butter over medium heat. Add the garlic and cook, stirring, until the garlic is fragrant and just begins to brown—about 30 seconds. Pour over the fried plantains and serve immediately.

Yield: 2 servings

Apple Fritters

Apple fritters are a delicious accompaniment to game, especially duck and duck confit, or ham. The sweetness and tart edge they offer are the perfect foils for rich-tasting, full-bodied meats. Of course, chicken or a pork chop wouldn't be insulted by such company, either. Don't worry too much if a sauce is to be involved, unless it is tomato based. Ideally, a cream or white-wine-based sauce is best, possibly flavored with garlic, a bit of ham, onion, or herbs.

As for other side dishes, I immediately think of greens—Kale with Bacon and Onion (page 127), for example, or Creamed Spinach (page 129).

1 egg	Pinch of cayenne pepper
1 tablespoon milk	A grating of nutmeg
4 teaspoons all-purpose flour, plus more for dredging	1 tart apple, such as Granny Smith
	Vegetable oil, for frying
Pinch of salt	

Combine the egg, milk, flour, and seasonings in a bowl. Mix well.

Place some flour for dredging in another bowl.

Peel and core the apple. Cut it crosswise into $\frac{1}{4}$-inch-thick slices.

Heat about $\frac{1}{2}$ inch of oil in a large skillet over moderate heat until a drop of the egg mixture immediately sizzles. Dredge the apple slices in the flour and then in the egg mixture. Fry the battered apple slices until golden brown, 1 to 2 minutes, and then turn and brown the other side. Regulate the heat so they don't brown too fast—the apple should be cooked through but still somewhat crunchy. Serve immediately.

Yield: about 6 fritters

NOTE: These fritters are also great for dessert with just a dusting of cinnamon sugar and maybe some vanilla ice cream.

Broccoli Tempura

Tempura is an irresistible way to cook vegetables and very tempting for children. The important things to know when preparing tempura batter are not to mix it too much (leave the lumps!) and to make the batter right before you need it.

Tempura seems like a lighthearted preparation, so serve it with more casual meals. Try Fried Rice with Spring Vegetables (page 29) or Parsnip Purée with Orange (page 42) with it.

Vegetable oil, for deep-frying	**2 egg yolks**
1 head broccoli	**2 cups all-purpose flour, plus more**
2 cups ice water	**for dredging**

Heat the oil to 375° F. in a heavy 3-quart saucepan.

Cut the broccoli into large flowerets.

Combine the ice water and egg yolks in a mixing bowl with a fork. Add all the flour all at once, and, using the fork, mix quickly and briefly, leaving lots of lumps.

Dredge the broccoli flowerets in flour and shake off the excess. Dip a few pieces in the batter and immediately drop them into the hot oil. Some of the batter will scatter around the edges of the pot—just skim it out as you tend the frying. Fry the broccoli until the batter is crisp and very light brown, about 2 minutes. Remove the tempura from the oil and let it drain on a rack over paper towels while you fry the rest. Don't pile the pieces of fried broccoli on top of one another or they will become soggy. Serve immediately.

Yield: 4 servings

Chinese-Style Dry-Fried Green Beans

This cooking method produces green beans that are quite flavorful and still crunchy. The light gingery stock enrobing each bean makes this dish a little more special than the usual sautéed green bean. When deciding on accompaniments, the element to consider is how the ginger will combine with other flavors on the plate. For instance, a preparation in which garlic is the main seasoning might be complemented nicely by the ginger, but one with red wine would not.

2 tablespoons vegetable oil	**½ cup chicken stock**
1½ teaspoons grated fresh ginger	**Salt to taste**
1 pound green beans, ends trimmed	

In a 12-inch skillet, heat the vegetable oil over high heat. Add the ginger and sauté, stirring, for 30 seconds.

Add the green beans and sauté for 3 minutes, tossing occasionally. Add the chicken stock and cook the green beans, tossing occasionally, until all the stock has evaporated and the beans are blistered and somewhat browned, 5 to 7 minutes. Season with salt and serve immediately.

Yield: 4 to 6 servings

Fried Zucchini with Black and White Sesame Seeds, Japanese Style

The dressing adds a slightly sweet dimension and the sesame seeds a pleasing color combination to basic fried zucchini. This goes particularly well with a light summer fish dish, but serve it with any entrée when the sweetness of the dressing won't interfere. The Japanese products called for in the recipe are available in Asian markets and many supermarkets.

FOR THE DRESSING

2 tablespoons mirin (Japanese sweet rice cooking wine)

2 tablespoons rice vinegar

1 teaspoon soy sauce, preferably Japanese

1 tablespoon white sesame seeds

1 tablespoon black sesame seeds

$\frac{1}{2}$ teaspoon salt

1 large zucchini

All-purpose flour, for dusting

Vegetable oil, for frying

Combine all the ingredients for the dressing in a small bowl and mix well. Set aside.

Cut the zucchini into thinish sticks, about $\frac{1}{4}$ inch by $\frac{1}{4}$ inch by $2\frac{1}{2}$ inches. Dust with the flour.

Heat several inches of vegetable oil to 375° F. in a heavy skillet. Fry the zucchini in batches until golden brown and quite crisp. Drain on paper towels while you fry the rest.

When all the zucchini is fried, mound it on a serving platter and drizzle it with the dressing. Serve immediately.

Yield: 2 to 4 servings

Grated Zucchini Cake

When preparing a delicate dish with feminine characteristics, such as sole with herbed beurre blanc or poached chicken breast with a light tomato cream, I look for a side dish that harmonizes with the style of the entrée. If your entrée has subtle flavors, the side dish must not overwhelm it in flavor or texture. This zucchini cake is perfect for these situations. The zucchini is fresh and naturally slightly sweet, and the vibrant green color is quite pretty.

1 large zucchini	**1 scallion, thinly sliced**
1 slice firm white bread, crusts removed	**A few grinds of black pepper**
	3 tablespoons olive oil
1 tablespoon kosher salt	

Grate the zucchini coarsely using the larger holes on your grater. Toss with the salt and place in a colander to drain for 15 minutes.

Place the bread in a blender or food processor and process until it is finely ground. Squeeze the zucchini to get rid of the excess moisture and combine it in a mixing bowl with the bread crumbs, scallion, and pepper.

In a 12-inch skillet, heat the olive oil over medium heat. Form the zucchini into four 3-inch patties and fry until golden brown, about 3 minutes. Turn once and brown the other side. Serve immediately.

Yield: 4 patties

Curried Vidalia Onion Fritters

These delicious fritters made of sweet Vidalia onions are crowd pleasers. I sometimes serve them as an hors d'oeuvre with a sweet-and-sour dipping sauce. They are also a great side dish. Try them alongside entrées with Middle Eastern or Asian seasonings as well as basic roasts and sautés. They go well with not only sweet-and-sour flavorings, but also spicy sauces.

The batter is thick, and if you fry the fritters right after adding the onions it will produce round, puffy fritters—make sure they are cooked through. I prefer to wait an hour or so and let the onion juices dilute the batter to make thinner, more spidery fritters. If you want the thinner kind and can't wait, just add a little more milk.

1 cup all-purpose flour	Dash of vinegar
Scant 1 teaspoon baking powder	A few dashes hot sauce
2 teaspoons curry powder	1 large Vidalia onion, peeled, cut
1 teaspoon salt	in half, and thinly sliced
1 cup milk	Vegetable oil, for frying
1 egg	

Mix all the dry ingredients together in a bowl.

Beat the liquids together. Pour over the dry ingredients and combine. Add the sliced onion and mix well. If possible, let stand for 1 hour.

In a large saucepan or deep skillet heat 3 inches of vegetable oil to 350° F. over medium heat.

Drop the batter into the hot oil by tablespoonfuls, being careful not to crowd the pan. Cook until browned on one side and then turn. When the fritters are deep golden brown all over, remove them and drain on paper towels. It's a good idea to break one open to test for doneness; if it is underdone in the center, reduce the heat a bit, and fry another minute. Repeat until all the batter is used up and serve immediately.

Yield: about 20 small fritters

Mashed Black Bean Cakes with Cilantro

Mashing beans as they do in South America is an enticing way to use leftover cooked beans, giving them a different texture and the possibility of incorporating flavorings. The cilantro is key here— make sure it has good flavor, as too often it can be almost tasteless. Grilled shrimp or firm-fleshed fish would pair very well, as would pork chops or chicken. Think of entrées seasoned with one or any combination of the following: garlic, chiles, onions, lime juice, and olive oil. The Tomato and Avocado Salsa (page 151) is a good partner for these black-bean cakes.

2 cups cooked black beans	1 small egg, lightly beaten
2 tablespoons coarsely chopped fresh cilantro	2 teaspoons all-purpose flour
1 garlic clove, minced	Salt and freshly ground pepper to taste
2 tablespoons thinly sliced scallion, green and white parts	Olive oil, for frying
	Cornmeal, for dredging

Mash the beans with a potato masher or an electric beater, or in a food processor. They don't have to be completely smooth—a few whole beans or semimashed ones are fine.

Add the cilantro, garlic, scallion, egg, flour, salt, and pepper and combine thoroughly. Form the bean mixture into flat cakes, about ¾ inch thick and 2½ inches in diameter.

In a sauté pan, heat about ¼ inch of oil over medium-high heat. Dredge the bean cakes in cornmeal and fry them in batches, without crowding, until crisped and browned on one side—about 3 minutes. Flip the cakes once and brown the other side. You may have to lower the heat a little to make sure the cakes are heated through and don't burn. Drain on paper towels and keep warm in a 200° F. oven while you are frying the rest Serve immediately.

Yield: 8 cakes

Hush Puppies

Hush puppies are a classic American side dish, very often served with fried catfish. They're also great with barbecue, smothered pork chops, or chicken. Greens such as Southern Collard Greens (page 128) would be just right alongside.

I like to fry the hush puppies in a 10-inch cast-iron skillet because I can cook about 10 at a time, and the heavy iron retains heat very well.

1 cup yellow cornmeal	Small pinch of cayenne pepper
¼ cup all-purpose flour	2 tablespoons minced onion
¼ teaspoon baking soda	1 egg
1 teaspoon baking powder	1 cup buttermilk
1½ teaspoons salt	1 quart vegetable oil, for frying
2 teaspoons sugar	

Combine the cornmeal, flour, baking soda, baking powder, salt, sugar, cayenne, and minced onion in a medium bowl, and whisk well.

Whisk together the egg and buttermilk and add to the dry ingredients. Whisk everything together until just combined.

Heat the vegetable oil to 350° F. Drop tablespoons of batter into the hot oil and fry until golden brown, about 3 minutes. Carefully break open a hush puppy (it will be extremely hot) to check for doneness. If it is still runny in the center, fry another minute. Drain the hush puppies on paper towels, then serve immediately.

Yield: about 30 2-inch hush puppies

NOTE: Hush puppies can be fried and then frozen in plastic bags. Reheat in a 350° F. oven for 10 minutes.

Crispy New England Corn Cakes with Scallions

These wonderful pancakes can go with just about anything, especially a shellfish dinner. You can vary them by adding finely diced red pepper or chopped herbs, for example.

1 cup all-purpose flour

¾ teaspoon baking powder

¼ teaspoon salt

A few gratings of nutmeg

Small pinch of cayenne pepper

4 grinds of black pepper

Dash of white wine vinegar

1 egg, beaten

½ to ¾ cup milk

2 tablespoons minced celery

2 tablespoons minced onion

2 cups fresh corn kernels (about 4 ears)

1 cup thinly sliced scallion, green and white parts

Vegetable oil, for frying

Sift together the all-purpose flour, baking powder, salt, nutmeg, cayenne, and black pepper into a bowl.

Beat together the vinegar, egg, and ½ cup of the milk. Stir this into the dry ingredients, but do not overmix. If the batter seems too stiff, add the remaining ¼ cup of milk.

Stir in the celery, onion, corn, and scallion.

In a 10-inch skillet, heat ¼ cup vegetable oil until hot. Spoon in the batter, making pancakes approximately 3 inches in diameter. Reduce the heat to medium and cook the pancakes until they are browned on the bottom and bubbles start to break on the surface. Flip the pancakes and brown the other side. Drain on paper towels and keep warm in a 200° F. oven while you fry the rest. Add a little more oil to the pan, if necessary, when you fry subsequent batches. Serve hot.

Yield: 12 fritters

Potato Fritters with Cornichons and Bacon

These fritters, inspired by a recipe of Georges Blanc, go well with all meats and firm fish, especially if there is a sauce or gravy to sop up. Serve them with a green vegetable.

3 Idaho potatoes	$\frac{1}{4}$ cup milk
6 strips bacon	Salt and freshly ground pepper
3 tablespoons potato starch	to taste
3 eggs	Olive or vegetable oil, for frying
3 egg whites	12 small cornichons, thinly sliced

Peel the potatoes, cut them in quarters, and place in a saucepan with salted water to cover. Bring to a boil and cook over moderately high heat until thoroughly cooked, about 20 minutes. Drain.

While the potatoes are boiling, cook the bacon in a skillet over medium heat until crisp. Drain the bacon and crumble it into $\frac{1}{4}$-inch pieces.

Purée the potatoes, either by putting them through a food mill or by whipping them with an electric beater. They must be smooth but not overprocessed or they will be gummy.

Put the potato purée in a bowl and mix in the potato starch, 1 tablespoon at a time, until the purée thickens. You may not need to add all the starch.

Beat in the eggs and egg whites, one at a time. Stir in the milk. The batter should be the consistency of pancake batter; if it seems too thick, add a little more milk. Add salt and pepper.

In a 10-inch sauté pan, heat about $\frac{1}{4}$ inch of oil over medium heat until a drop of batter sizzles on contact. Add the potato batter by the spoonful to make 3-inch fritters, cooking 3 at a time. Sprinkle some cornichons and bacon on top. Adjust the heat so they don't cook too fast—they should turn a nice golden brown (about 2 minutes). Flip the fritters once and cook until done. Remove the fritters to a plate lined with paper towels and place in a 200° F. oven while you cook the rest. Serve hot.

Yield: about 12 fritters

Potato Cake with Scallion

This potato cake, crispy on the outside and creamy inside, is sometimes referred to as "rosti." The trick to a good potato cake is monitoring the speed at which you cook it—too fast and it will brown unevenly, too slow and it will turn gray before it's done. Steady moderate heat and a good amount of butter or oil are needed to produce that golden-brown crust, which is the whole reason for making a potato cake. Serve it with just about anything.

2 large Idaho potatoes, peeled	A few grinds of black pepper
5 scallions, thinly sliced	2 tablespoons unsalted butter
1 teaspoon salt	1 tablespoon olive oil

Shred the potatoes and place them in a bowl. Add the scallions, salt, and pepper and toss to combine.

Heat a heavy 10-inch sauté pan over medium heat until hot. Add the butter and oil. When the foam subsides, add the potato mixture to the pan, pressing with a spatula to form a flat cake. Adjust the heat so there is some bubbling action, but don't let the cake brown too quickly. Cook the potato cake for 15 to 20 minutes on the first side, at which point it should be golden brown and crispy.

Turn the potato cake over and cook it on the second side for another 15 minutes. You may have to add more oil or butter to the pan when you turn the cake over if the pan looks too dry. An easy way to flip the cake is to invert it onto a plate and then slide it back into the pan. Cut the potato cake into wedges and serve immediately.

Yield: 4 servings

Curried Potato Chips

Potato chips in the form of pommes gaufrettes *(waffle chips) are a classic French accompaniment to game. This version has a mild curry flavoring, which gives the chips a little verve. They are great with sandwiches and summer salads as well as alongside a dinner entrée. Grilled foods immediately come to mind, but consider them with almost any roasted or sautéed meat or fish. I would avoid serving them with starchy entrées, such as pasta or meat stews with potatoes already in them.*

You can use a regular frying pan or a tabletop deep fryer to fry the chips. Be sure to stir them often as they cook because they like to stick together.

1 large Idaho potato	**2 teaspoons mild curry powder**
1 cup vegetable oil, for frying	**¼ teaspoon salt**
1 garlic clove, very finely minced	

Peel the potato if you wish—it is not necessary. Slice it very thin with a mandolin or knife and put the slices in a colander. Rinse them with cold water and dry them between paper towels.

Heat the vegetable oil in a 10-inch skillet to about 350° F. You will know it's hot enough when a potato slice sizzles on contact.

Fry the chips in batches, 5 or 6 at a time, and keep them moving as they cook to make sure they brown evenly and don't stick. When they turn golden brown, use tongs or a slotted spoon to remove the chips to paper towels to drain.

When all the chips are fried, place them in a bowl. Place about 1 tablespoon of the hot frying oil in a small bowl, add the garlic and let it sit for 30 seconds. Add the curry powder and salt and stir well. Drizzle this mixture over the chips and toss very gently to coat all the chips. Serve warm or at room temperature.

Yield: 2 to 4 servings

Baked Potato Chips

I'm not totally convinced that this method produces a chip that is lower in fat, but it's possible that it does. To my mind, the two main advantages of this method are that you don't need to use a whole pot of cooking oil and that the potato chips come out absolutely flat. This last point is fun sometimes when you want to make a special presentation on a plate—standing them upright in a purée, for example. Flavorings like garlic or herbs can be added before the chips go in the oven.

1 large Idaho potato	**Salt to taste**
Vegetable oil, for brushing	

Preheat the oven to 350° F.

Peel the potatoes or don't as you wish. Slice them very thin and even, using a mandolin if you have one.

Lightly but thoroughly grease a sheet pan. Lay the potato slices on the sheet pan close but not touching. Gently brush the chips with a little oil.

Lightly sprinkle some salt over the chips and bake for about 10 minutes, until golden brown. Monitor the baking closely—you will probably have to rotate the pan to ensure more even cooking. Also, some chips will cook faster than others, so just remove them from the sheet pan as they're done. Use a metal spatula to lift the chips off the sheet pan while they are still hot. Let cool before serving.

Yield: 2 to 4 servings

Barbecue-Flavored French Fries

These fries fall into the category of fun food. Homemade fries are always great, and the spice mix added here makes them somewhat whimsical. I wouldn't serve them at too serious a meal—save them for an outdoor barbecue or a simple meal of sandwiches or plain chicken.

For great fries, try to find a long potato. This method may seem somewhat unorthodox, but I assure you it results in greaseless, crispy french fries. The frying oil can be reused several times if you let it cool down to room temperature, filter it through a fine-meshed strainer, and store it in an airtight container, refrigerated.

1 large Idaho potato	**1 teaspoon Barbecue Powder**
1 quart vegetable oil, for frying	**(page 192)**

The potato may be peeled or not, depending on your preference. Cut the potato into french fries the length of your potato and ¼ inch by ¼ inch. Place in a bowl, cover with cold water, and soak for at least 1 hour.

Place the oil in a deep saucepan and heat to 275° F. Drain the french fries and dry them with paper towels. Fry them in 3 or 4 batches, without crowding, until the potatoes have become flexible and somewhat translucent, about 5 minutes. You do not want to brown them at this stage. Spread the now-blanched french fries out on a plate.

Raise the temperature of the oil to 375° F. Refry the potatoes in batches until golden and crispy, about 3 minutes. As they come out of the oil, place them in a large mixing bowl. When they are all fried, beautiful, and crispy, sprinkle on the Barbecue Powder and toss. Serve immediately.

Yield: 2 servings

Simple Sides

Side dishes do not have to be complicated or use expensive ingredients to be great. Often, simplicity is called for, whether the side is meant to show off a complex entrée or to highlight fine fresh ingredients. When sugar snaps are at their best, for example, you just want to accent their sweetness rather than overwhelm them with a heavy spice or sauce. Other preparations serve to intensify a flavor, as with Roasted Garlic Cloves.

Many of the recipes in this chapter are standbys, the ones that I prepare often for everyday meals. They are versatile in their application and are sure to please.

Marinated Beefsteak Tomatoes ◆ *Caramelized Garlic* ◆ *Roasted Garlic Cloves* ◆ *Poached Pears in Sweet Wine* ◆ *Glazed Onions* ◆ *Buttered Zucchini Ribbons* ◆ *Grilled Radicchio with Smoked Mozzarella* ◆ *Husk-Roasted Corn* ◆ *Barley Pilaf* ◆ *Vegetable Barley* ◆ *Roasted New Potatoes with Garlic* ◆ *Steamed New Potatoes with Mint* ◆ *Boiled New Potatoes with Onion and Gruyère, Savoie Style* ◆ *Cauliflower Gratin with Gruyère* ◆ *Cauliflower Polonaise*

Marinated Beefsteak Tomatoes

You could use any firm, fleshy tomato for this preparation, but large beefsteaks make an impressive presentation. Don't even think about trying this recipe unless tomatoes are in season and you've got one that's actually ripe.

These tomatoes are divine with roast beef or grilled steaks, chicken, and firm seafood such as tuna, swordfish, monkfish or shrimp. Baby New Potato Salad with Bacon and Chives (page 165) or Warm Curried Lentil Salad (page 157) would be just right alongside.

1 large ripe beefsteak tomato	**Salt and freshly ground pepper**
3 tablespoons balsamic vinegar	**to taste**
2 tablespoons extra virgin olive oil	**1 tablespoon shredded fresh basil**

Cut the tomato into ½-inch slices.

In a medium bowl, whisk together the vinegar, olive oil, salt, pepper, and basil. Add the tomato slices to the dressing and marinate for 1 hour before serving.

Yield: 2 servings

NOTE: The tomatoes may be prepared a day ahead of time and kept in the refrigerator, but bring them back to room temperature before serving.

Caramelized Garlic

This recipe and the one that follows are more accents than true side dishes, but they are both delicious and addictive!

Boiling garlic gives it a mild, sweet character and caramelization does even more so. Serve Caramelized Garlic to highlight any meat or aggressive fish. It is particularly good with pork, chicken, or game.

8 whole garlic cloves	**½ teaspoon sugar**
1 teaspoon clarified butter	**Small pinch of salt**
(see Note)	

Carefully peel the garlic, leaving the cloves unbroken. Place them in a small saucepan and cover them with cold water. Place the pot over high heat and bring to a boil. Lower the heat and simmer the garlic for 10 to 15 minutes, until it is cooked through and soft but not mushy. Drain.

Heat an 8-inch sauté pan over high heat until very hot. Add the butter and garlic and sauté, tossing continually for 10 seconds. Add the sugar and continue tossing until the sugar has caramelized and the garlic is a dark golden brown—be careful not to burn it. Sprinkle with salt and immediately remove the garlic from the pan. Serve immediately.

Yield: 2 servings

NOTE: Clarified butter has a higher burning point than whole butter, because the milk solids have been removed. Clarified butter can be made by gently melting unsalted butter and skimming off the white solids that rise to the top. Gently ladle off the clear butter into a storage container, leaving behind the water at the bottom, which has separated out. You will have to clarify at least $\frac{1}{4}$ pound, but you can store the clarified butter indefinitely in the refrigerator. It is great to use for sautéing fish and vegetables.

Roasted Garlic Cloves

Roasting garlic gives it an intense, sweet, and mellow flavor. You can enjoy the cloves whole, as a side, or peel and mash them onto bread for a snack.

1 head garlic	**Salt and freshly ground pepper**
Olive oil	**to taste**

Preheat the oven to 350° F.

Separate the cloves and peel them without breaking them. Toss them with enough olive oil to coat, sprinkle them with salt and pepper, and wrap them loosely in foil.

Bake the garlic, turning the package over once, for 30 to 45 minutes or until the garlic is fragrant and soft.

Yield: 2 to 4 servings

Poached Pears in Sweet Wine

This version of poached pears is more delicate and subtle than Spiced Poached Pears in Red Wine (page 102). Serve it with your daintier birds.

2 cups sweet white wine, such as a late-harvest Riesling	**1-inch strip orange zest** **2 ripe pears**

Combine the wine and orange zest in a deep nonreactive pot.

Peel the pears. Slice them in half lengthwise and remove the core. Place the pears in the pot with the wine. Bring them to a boil over high heat and then reduce the heat to maintain a gentle simmer. Poach the pears for about 35 minutes or until tender. Test for doneness by piercing a pear with a toothpick, which should go in easily. Gently remove the pears from the liquid. If you are not serving them immediately, cool the poaching liquid and cover the pears with it.

Yield: 4 servings

N O T E : Poached pears may be served hot, cold, or at room temperature. They are very pretty when sliced lengthwise and fanned on the plate.

Glazed Onions

This basic side dish is extremely versatile, going well with any kind of meat, from an honest roast chicken to an elegant noisette of venison.

Glazed onions seem to me to be an autumnal dish, so I keep that in mind when choosing another side to pair them with. This leaves plenty to choose from—just avoid those dishes that have a similar texture or sweetness.

10 small white onions **1 tablespoon clarified butter** **(page 79)**	**1½ teaspoons sugar** **Salt to taste**

Peel the onions and blanch them in boiling water for approximately 20 minutes or until a toothpick can easily be inserted into the center of an onion. Drain well.

Heat a 10-inch skillet over high heat until very hot. Add the clarified butter and heat for 15 seconds. Add the onions and sauté, tossing continually for 1 minute. Sprinkle with the sugar and salt and continue tossing until the sugar has caramelized and become golden brown. Serve immediately.

Yield: 2 to 4 servings

Buttered Zucchini Ribbons

Zucchini ribbons are sometimes also referred to as "zucchini noodles," because the zucchini is cut in a way that resembles strips of pasta. To cut zucchini ribbons, you need to have a device known as a mandolin. If you do a moderate amount of cooking at home, this is a worthwhile tool to have for the ease with which you can shred, julienne, and thinly slice vegetables.

Zucchini ribbons are simple in preparation and flavor, making them an easy match for all sorts of main courses. The long, thin, flat strips are very attractive on the plate.

1 medium zucchini	**½ teaspoon chopped mixed light**
1 tablespoon unsalted butter,	**fresh herbs, such as chervil,**
softened	**parsley, chives (optional)**
Salt and freshly ground pepper	
to taste	

Trim the ends from the zucchini and slice it into thin ribbons using the mandolin's wider french-fry blade. Place the ribbons in an 8-inch sauté pan with ½ cup of water and a pinch of salt. Bring the water to a boil over high heat and cook the zucchini until just done and bright green, about 2 minutes.

Drain the zucchini ribbons and place them in a serving bowl with the softened butter, salt, pepper, and herbs if using. Toss gently and serve immediately.

Yield: 2 servings

Grilled Radicchio with Smoked Mozzarella

This dish is so simple, yet absolutely delicious. It is best made over a wood fire, but, lacking one, I wouldn't hesitate to use an oven broiler.

If you have some garlic oil (made from macerating chopped garlic in olive oil), use it for brushing the radicchio. Serve the grilled radicchio with hot or cold pastas, tuna, swordfish, shrimp, chicken, or veal. Sautéed Mushrooms with Oregano (page 8) is a perfect companion.

1 nice large head radicchio	**2 ½-inch-thick slices smoked**
Olive oil, for brushing	**mozzarella**
Salt and freshly ground pepper	
to taste	

Have ready a moderately hot charcoal or wood fire or preheat the broiler for 10 minutes.

Trim off the browned edge of the radicchio stem and cut the head in half lengthwise. Brush the halves generously with olive oil and sprinkle with salt and pepper.

Grill the radicchio, cut side down, until it starts to wilt and looks brown and a bit charred around the edges, about 5 minutes depending on the heat of your fire. Turn the radicchio and top each half with a slice of smoked mozzarella. The cheese will melt as the other side cooks. Remove the radicchio from the fire when the cheese has melted and the lettuce is hot all the way through. Serve immediately.

Yield: 2 servings

NOTE: If using a broiler, broil the radicchio on both sides until done and then top with the cheese. Melt the cheese under the broiler until lightly browned and serve.

Husk-Roasted Corn

For this recipe you must have absolutely fresh corn, which, luckily for many city dwellers, is available at farmer's markets these days. Serve this at any feast. If you have already fired up the barbecue, wrap the ears in foil and bury them in the embers.

4 ears fresh corn

8 tablespoons Herb Butter (see page 194), softened

Preheat the oven to 425°F.

Gently pull down the husks of each ear, leaving them attached at the bottom. Remove the corn silk. Pull the husks back up over the corn and soak the ears in cold water for 30 minutes (this is to prevent the husk from burning).

Remove the corn from the water and pat the ears dry. Gently pull down the husks again and rub each ear all over with 2 tablespoons of herb butter. Replace the husks, wrap the ears individually in foil, and roast them for about 35 minutes. Take 1 ear out of the oven and peek at the corn—it should still be crunchy. Discard the foil and serve immediately.

Yield: 4 servings

Barley Pilaf

This basic barley recipe can be the starting point for other preparations. I like to have cooked barley on hand to reheat at the last minute for an impromptu meal. These proportions produce al dente barley—if you prefer a softer grain, increase the stock by $1/2$ cup.

1 tablespoon unsalted butter	Salt and freshly ground pepper
2 tablespoons chopped onion	to taste
2 cups uncooked pearled barley	1 bay leaf
2 cups chicken stock	

In a heavy-bottomed $1\frac{1}{2}$-quart saucepan, melt the butter over medium-low heat. Add the onion and sweat for a few minutes, until it is softened but not brown.

Add the barley and stir well to coat each grain with butter. Cook the barley this way for a minute or two, until it starts to turn opaque. Add the stock, salt, pepper, and bay leaf and bring to a boil over high heat. Reduce the heat to low, cover tightly, and simmer very gently for about 35 to 40 minutes, until all the stock is absorbed. Taste the barley, adjust the seasonings, remove the bay leaf, and fluff with a fork before serving.

Yield: 4 to 6 servings

Vegetable Barley

Serve this dish with any meat or fish, although it is particularly nice with game. The vegetables may be varied as you wish, substituting broccoli, turnips, scallion, or peppers, for example. This is a wonderful way to use leftover cooked barley.

1 cup uncooked pearled barley	¼ cup diced zucchini
1 tablespoon vegetable or olive oil	¼ cup diced carrots
1½ tablespoons diced onion	1 tablespoon soy sauce
½ cup diced mushrooms	Salt to taste

In a 2-quart saucepan, combine the barley with 4 cups of water. Bring to a boil and then reduce the heat to keep the water at a low boil until the barley is cooked, about 20 minutes. Stir the barley occasionally while it is cooking to prevent it from sticking to the pan's bottom. Drain.

In an 8-inch skillet, heat the oil over medium heat. Add the onion, mushrooms, zucchini, and carrots. Sauté, stirring often, until lightly browned and just cooked, about 5 minutes. Add the cooked barley and stir to combine.

Season with the soy sauce and salt and serve.

Yield: 2 to 4 servings

Roasted New Potatoes with Garlic

This is one of the side dishes I prepare most frequently. It's simple, highly pleasing, and goes with just about everything. The potatoes are truly best when prepared with duck fat, but butter or olive oil gives excellent results as well. The trick is to use a preheated heavy pan—a cast-iron skillet works best. Lacking one, use the heaviest sheet pan or pie pan you have and don't crowd the potatoes.

1½ tablespoons rendered duck fat, unsalted butter, or olive oil	Salt and freshly ground pepper to taste
6 red new potatoes	3 garlic cloves, minced

Place a 10-inch cast-iron skillet with the fat of your choice in a preheated oven at 400° F. for 10 minutes.

Quarter the new potatoes lengthwise to form wedges. Place them in the preheated skillet, sprinkle with the salt and pepper, and stir to coat the potatoes with the hot fat. Roast for 15 minutes.

Add the garlic and stir everything up. Continue roasting for another 10 to 15 minutes, until the potatoes are cooked through and are crisp and browned.

Yield: 2 servings

NOTE: These potatoes may be prepared a bit ahead of time and then popped back into the oven to reheat and recrisp.

Steamed New Potatoes with Mint

This is an uncomplicated dish with light, refreshing flavors, suitable for serving with delicate fish, poached chicken, shellfish, or crustaceans. Pair it with something equally simple, perhaps some steamed snow peas or sautéed string beans.

8 small new potatoes	1½ teaspoons unsalted butter
1 heaping tablespoon coarsely chopped fresh mint	½ teaspoon kosher salt

Steam the potatoes over simmering water until done, about 30 to 40 minutes, depending on their size.

Place the potatoes in a bowl and add the mint, butter, and salt. Toss until the butter has melted and serve immediately.

Yield: 2 to 4 servings

Boiled New Potatoes with Onion and Gruyère, Savoie Style

This dish was inspired by memories of raclette, a dish popular in the Alps. A large wheel of cheese is placed up against a lit fireplace, its flames melting the cheese while the aroma penetrates. The melted cheese is then ceremoniously scraped off onto a plate of boiled potatoes and/or charcuterie. Actually, these days you are more likely to encounter a small electrical appliance that is brought to your table, in which you can broil slices of cheese in a small cast-iron skillet and scrape it onto your plate with a wooden paddle. It's still lots of fun, even without the fragrance of a wood-burning fire.

While somewhat further removed from the original inspiration, the following recipe is nevertheless a satisfying and comforting dish for cold weather. Serve it with roast beef, ham, or chicken.

16 small new potatoes	**Salt and freshly ground pepper**
1 onion, peeled and thinly sliced	**to taste**
	¼ pound sliced Gruyère cheese

Place the potatoes in a 3-quart saucepan and cover them with cold, salted water. Bring the potatoes to a boil over high heat and cook them until tender, about 30 minutes. Drain.

Cut the potatoes into halves or quarters while they are still hot. Place them on an oven-proof serving platter and sprinkle the onion slices on top. Season with the salt and pepper and top with the slices of Gruyère cheese. Broil for 2 to 3 minutes, until the cheese is melted, bubbly, and lightly browned. Serve immediately.

Yield: 4 servings

Cauliflower Gratin with Gruyère

This is a recipe for cauliflower lovers. The cheese has an assertive flavor, so serve this dish with entrées for which that won't be a problem. Some steamed greens would complete the plate.

1 head cauliflower
1 to 1½ cups Béchamel Sauce
  (page 191)

⅛ pound sliced Gruyère

Preheat the oven to 400° F.

Cut the cauliflower into flowerets. Blanch them in boiling salted water until tender, about 10 minutes. Drain and pat dry.

Place the cooked cauliflower in a 6-cup gratin dish. Pour the béchamel over the cauliflower, and arrange the slices of cheese on top. Bake for 15 to 20 minutes, until the gratin is hot and bubbling and the cheese has melted.

Place the cooked gratin under the broiler for 2 to 3 minutes to brown the top. Serve immediately.

Yield: 4 servings

Cauliflower Polonaise

This is an old-fashioned French dish of the Escoffier variety. I adore the polonaise preparation, which is also suitable for asparagus, green beans, or broccoli. I have even used it with ravioli. Serve it with chicken, veal, pork, fish (especially flounder fillet), or game.

Steamed greens or green beans would make an appropriate second side.

1 head cauliflower	Salt and freshly ground pepper
Dash of vinegar	to taste
2 eggs	5 tablespoons unsalted butter
$\frac{1}{4}$ cup chopped fresh parsley	1 cup fresh bread crumbs
$\frac{1}{2}$ teaspoon minced garlic	

Cut the cauliflower into flowerets. Blanch them in boiling salted water for about 10 minutes or until tender. Drain and pat dry.

While the cauliflower is cooking, bring a quart of water to a boil. Add a dash of vinegar and gently lower the eggs into the water. Lower the heat to a steady simmer and cook the eggs for 12 minutes. Drain, then cool the hard-boiled eggs under cold water.

When cool, peel the eggs and chop them coarsely. Combine them in a bowl with the parsley, garlic, salt, and pepper.

Place the hot cauliflower in a shallow serving bowl or arrange on a platter. Sprinkle with the egg mixture.

Melt the butter in a small skillet over high heat. When it is lightly browned, add the bread crumbs and toss rapidly. Pour the buttered crumbs over the cauliflower and serve immediately.

Yield: 4 servings

Extravagant Sides

The recipes in this chapter are for those occasions when you want to make an extra effort. The simplest roast meat or sautéed fish can be gussied up by a fancy side dish. Side dishes go a long way in deciding the complexion of a meal, and they say a lot about the message you are trying to convey with food. Sides can tell your guests or family that it is a special occasion, that you went to some trouble, or that they can have fun and relax.

Some sides can be classified as extravagant from the obvious luxury of the ingredients, as with Wild Mushrooms with Brandy and Cream. Other times food is rendered fancy by the work involved in preparing it and by the final appearance of the dish. The Zucchini and Carrot Terrine is made with fairly inexpensive ingredients, yet the beauty of the alternating layers of green and yellow and the technique involved make it unique. Often, a side can be fairly simple or easy to prepare, but just looks special, as in Zucchini Blossoms Filled with Lemoned Goat Cheese. This dish is also an example of a side that uses a more exotic or unexpected vegetable that makes the meal memorable just by its presence on the plate.

But even if these sides are not necessarily more expensive or more difficult to prepare, they will subtly impart an air of distinction to your menu.

Wild Mushrooms with Brandy and Cream ◆ *Shiitake Mushrooms with Madeira* ◆ *Broiled Stuffed Mushroom Caps with Parmesan* ◆ *Mushrooms à la Grecque* ◆ *Mushroom Strudel* ◆ *Eggplant Timbale* ◆ *Eggplant with Roasted Red Pepper* ◆ *Wild Rice Crepes with Apples and Chestnuts* ◆ *Spiced Poached Pears in Red Wine* ◆ *Cranberry Compote with Red Wine and Sweet Spices* ◆ *Provençal Tart* ◆ *Ratatouille Beggar's Purses* ◆ *Broccoli Strudel* ◆ *Herbed Asparagus Timbale* ◆ *Zucchini and Carrot Terrine* ◆ *Zucchini Blossoms Filled with Lemoned Goat Cheese* ◆ *Swiss Chard Tart* ◆ *Ramps with Mushrooms and Egg Noodles* ◆ *Tomato Risotto* ◆ *Creamy Rice with Feta* ◆ *Saffron Pilaf with Almonds and Raisins* ◆ *Curried Couscous with Pine Nuts and Currants* ◆ *Mushroom Ravioli* ◆ *Ratatouille Ravioli* ◆

Wild Mushrooms with Brandy and Cream

Wild mushrooms are increasingly available, both in upscale supermarkets and at farmer's markets. Actually, many of these mushrooms are not wild at all, but wild varieties that are now cultivated. For true wild mushrooms you must either find them yourself (which is not recommended unless you absolutely know what you are doing) or find a specialty source, of which there are quite a few.

At any rate, the cultivated varieties are wonderful, and with some searching, depending on the season, you should be able to come up with several varieties. But be warned: they are not cheap.

This recipe is best for a more formal or luxurious meal. Wild mushrooms have an intense earthiness that I find too strong in combination with some meats like lamb or even duck. However, they are sublime with lighter meats like chicken, guinea hen, veal, or pork. Beef is fine too, since I consider it fairly neutral. Some seafood works well, such as oysters, monkfish, shrimp, snapper, or bass.

For another side to serve with this recipe, simple asparagus would be perfect, as would string beans. Some buttered noodles or a Potato Cake with Scallion (page 70) would round things off nicely.

Approximately 4 cups raw mixed
  wild mushrooms (2 cups after
  sweating—see Note)
	⅔ cup heavy cream
	Salt and freshly ground pepper
	  to taste

1 tablespoon unsalted butter	Squeeze of fresh lemon juice
1 tablespoon olive oil	2 teaspoons chopped mixed light
½ teaspoon minced garlic	fresh herbs, such as parsley,
1 teaspoon minced shallot	chives, chervil (optional)
2 tablespoons brandy	

Trim the mushrooms of any tough stems. Wipe each one with a damp paper towel to remove grit and dirt. If the mushrooms are particularly dirty, give them a quick dunk in cold water. Wipe dry.

Slice or quarter the mushrooms. (It's nice to slice one variety and quarter another to add diversity to the dish.) Place the mushrooms with the butter in a skillet large enough to hold them all and sweat them gently over low heat. Stir occasionally. When the mushrooms have wilted, about 15 minutes, drain them. Reserve the liquid for another use—it's delicious.

Heat the olive oil in a 10-inch skillet over high heat. Add the mushrooms and sauté them, stirring until slightly browned, about 2 minutes. Add the garlic and shallot and sauté another minute, stirring. Don't let the garlic and shallot burn.

Remove the pan from the heat and add the brandy; the brandy will ignite, so be careful and stand back as you do this. Return the pan to the heat (if the brandy hasn't ignited already, it will now) and cook rapidly until the brandy has almost evaporated—about 15 seconds.

Add the cream, salt, and pepper and reduce the cream over high heat until a light, sauce-like consistency is achieved—about 1 minute. Add a squeeze of lemon and the herbs if desired and serve.

Yield: 2 servings

NOTE: It is difficult to say exactly the quantity of mushrooms you should start with to get 2 cups after sweating, since varieties have differing water contents. Figure at least twice that amount, and more for some varieties like oyster mushrooms.

Shiitake Mushrooms with Madeira

This mushroom dish is quick to prepare and excellent with beef or chicken. Madeira has an affinity for mushrooms; its sweetness mingles with the earthy mushrooms nicely.

10 fresh shiitake mushrooms	**¼ cup Rainwater Madeira**
1 tablespoon plus 1 teaspoon	**Salt and freshly ground pepper**
unsalted butter	**to taste**

Remove and discard the stems from the mushrooms and wipe the caps with a damp cloth. Slice the mushrooms into ½-inch strips.

In a 10-inch sauté pan, melt 1 tablespoon of the butter over medium-low heat. Add the mushrooms and cook, stirring frequently, until they are soft and cooked through, about 5 minutes.

Add the Madeira and the remaining teaspoon of butter. Raise the heat to high and cook until the Madeira and butter have reduced and coated the mushrooms. Season with salt and pepper and serve immediately.

Yield: 2 servings

Broiled Stuffed Mushroom Caps with Parmesan

This preparation intensifies the flavor of the mushrooms, making them an ideal accompaniment for beef. Chicken (perhaps with a garlic sauce), pork, or veal would also be wonderful. These mushrooms also make a great hors d'oeuvre. They may be prepared ahead of time and then heated and broiled at the last moment. Serve them with something very green, like spinach or green beans.

1 10-ounce box cultivated button mushrooms

3 teaspoons fresh lemon juice

½ teaspoon kosher salt

½ cup water

2 tablespoons unsalted butter, at room temperature

1 tablespoon minced shallot

1 garlic clove, minced

1 slice firm white bread, crusts removed and ground into crumbs in a blender or food processor

3 tablespoons grated Parmesan

¼ teaspoon dried thyme

⅛ teaspoon dried oregano

Grind of black pepper

Clean the mushrooms by wiping them with a damp towel. Remove the entire stem and reserve. Place the mushroom caps, open side down, in a 10-inch nonreactive skillet with 1 teaspoon of the lemon juice, ¼ teaspoon of the salt, and the water. Bring the water to a boil and then gently simmer the caps for about 20 minutes, until cooked through. Remove the mushroom caps to paper towels and let them cool, open side down. Discard the cooking liquid or save for a soup or sauce.

While the caps are simmering, trim and finely chop the reserved stems—you should get about 1 cup.

In a small saucepan, melt 1 tablespoon of the butter over low heat. Add the chopped mushroom stems, shallot, and garlic. Sweat over low heat for about 25 minutes, until the mushroom liquid has evaporated and the mixture is quite soft. Remove the mixture to a mixing bowl and let cool.

Preheat the oven to 375° F.

Add the bread crumbs, the remaining 2 teaspoons of lemon juice, 1 tablespoon of the Parmesan, the remaining tablespoon butter, thyme, oregano, the remaining ¼ teaspoon salt, and the pepper to the sautéed mushroom stems and combine thoroughly.

Fill the mushroom caps with the mixture, mounding it nicely. Sprinkle the remaining Parmesan over the stuffed caps. Place the mushrooms in a buttered baking dish and bake for 15 minutes. Remove the mushrooms from the oven and raise the oven temperature to broil. Place them under the broiler until golden brown. Serve immediately.

Yield: 4 servings

Mushrooms à la Grecque

Herbaceous and piquant, these mushrooms are delicious with grilled fish. Try them also with steak or chicken. As a second side dish, either Mashed Potato Casserole (page 39) or Baked Acorn Squash (page 17) would do nicely.

2 cups white wine	**15 whole black peppercorns**
½ cup olive oil	**⅛ teaspoon hot red pepper flakes**
1 tablespoon fresh lemon juice	**½ teaspoon salt**
3 bay leaves	**1 10-ounce box cultivated button**
1½ teaspoons dried oregano	**mushrooms**
1 teaspoon dried thyme	

Combine the wine, oil, lemon juice, bay leaves, oregano, thyme, peppercorns, red pepper flakes, and salt in a 2-quart nonreactive saucepan. Bring to a boil and then simmer gently for 5 minutes.

While the marinade is simmering, clean the mushrooms by wiping gently with a damp paper towel. Trim the stem ends and then cut the mushrooms in half or quarters, depending on their size.

Add the mushrooms to the simmering liquid and cook until just tender, 10 to 15 minutes. Serve hot or cold.

Yield: 2 to 4 servings

N O T E : These mushrooms keep indefinitely in the refrigerator and can also be served as an appetizer or in salads.

Mushroom Strudel

This elegant savory strudel contains a creamy mushroom filling encircled by light, crispy phyllo. Serve it next to any dish you like mushrooms with, keeping in mind the tone of this side. It would be distinguished next to a filet mignon, a special chicken dish, duck, or fillet of sole in a light herb sauce. As a second side dish, consider those that provide a textural contrast—Buttered Zucchini Ribbons (page 81), Sautéed Barley with Duck Fat and Kale (page 130), or Braised Leeks (page 20), for example.

2 10-ounce boxes cultivated button mushrooms	**Juice of ½ lemon**
	A few gratings of nutmeg
2 tablespoons unsalted butter	**Salt and freshly ground pepper to taste**
2 tablespoons olive oil	
½ cup finely diced onion	**1 tablespoon sour cream**
⅛ teaspoon dried thyme	**3 sheets phyllo dough**

Wipe the mushrooms with a damp towel. Cut them in half and place them in the bowl of a food processor. Pulse the machine until the mushrooms are finely chopped but not mushy.

Over medium-low heat, melt the butter with the olive oil in a 10-inch skillet. Pour off half of the butter–olive oil mixture into a small bowl and reserve. Add the onion and mushrooms to the skillet and sweat slowly, stirring occasionally, until all the moisture from the mushrooms has evaporated—about 20 minutes.

Add the thyme, lemon juice, nutmeg, salt, pepper, and sour cream. Mix well, taste, and adjust the seasonings. Cool to room temperature. Preheat the oven to 350° F.

Spread a sheet of phyllo on a work surface, with the short side facing you. Brush lightly with the reserved butter–olive oil mixture. Lay another sheet on top of the first sheet and lightly brush that one, too. Lay a final sheet on top and brush it. Cut the phyllo in half, crosswise. Mound ½ of the mushroom mixture on the edge of the phyllo nearest you. Roll it up, and place it on a greased sheet pan, seam side down. Repeat with the remaining mushroom filling and phyllo. Brush the tops with more butter–olive oil mixture and bake for about 25 minutes, until golden brown.

To serve, cut the strudels on the diagonal into 2-inch lengths. Serve them upright or cut side down on the plate.

Yield: 4 to 6 servings

Eggplant Timbale

According to Larousse, a timbale is a molded dish that is lined with pastry and contains meat, force-meats, and the like. Today, correctly or not, chefs refer to any small molded custards as "timbales." They make lovely side dishes and can be made with many vegetables. This eggplant one is perfect with lamb, as well as chicken, tuna, swordfish, or grilled sardines. Think of Provençale flavors as season-ings for your entrée—thyme, rosemary, lavender, tomatoes, onion, garlic, anchovy, olives.

As a second side dish, I would try to offset the creaminess of the timbale with something of firmer texture; Curried Potato Chips (page 71) or Sautéed Escarole with Garlic and Lemon (page 25) are possibilities. Also, Roasted Garlic Cloves (page 79) would add a nice accent.

1 medium eggplant	1 egg yolk
Olive oil	Salt and freshly ground pepper
½ cup milk	to taste
1 egg	Pinch of ground cumin

Preheat the oven to 350° F.

Rub the eggplant with olive oil, loosely wrap it in foil, and bake it until very soft. This may take some time, maybe as long as 2 hours. Reduce the oven temperature to 300° F. When the eggplant is cool enough to handle, peel off the skin. Purée the eggplant pulp in a food processor until very smooth. Measure ½ cup of purée, reserving any extra for another purpose. Cool the purée to room temperature.

Return the eggplant purée to the processor bowl and add the milk, egg, egg yolk, salt, pepper, and cumin. Process until well mixed.

Grease four 4-ounce molds with olive oil. Divide the custard mix among the molds. Place the molds in a roasting pan filled ⅔ of the way up the sides of the ramekins with tepid water, and bake for about an hour. The custards are done when they are just set in the center—don't let them puff.

Remove the custards from the water bath and let rest a few minutes. Invert each custard either directly onto a plate or onto a spatula and then slide it onto the plate.

Yield: 4 servings

N O T E : These timbales may be made a few days ahead. Let them cool in the molds, wrap them well, and refrigerate. Reheat in a 350° F. oven for 10 minutes, then unmold as above.

Eggplant with Roasted Red Pepper

This eggplant dish is nice and soft and would complement a crisp cutlet well. Try it also with veal or pork chops or a sautéed pasta dish made with olive oil. It needs a second side dish with some firm texture, such as Asparagus Almandine (page 11) or Sugar Snaps with Mint Gremolata (page 14).

1 large eggplant	½ teapoon dried thyme
Kosher salt	2 teaspoons dried oregano
1 tablespoon olive oil	¼ teaspoon hot red pepper flakes
1 tablespoon minced garlic	Salt to taste
½ a small onion, sliced	1 large red bell pepper
1 cup chicken stock	Squeeze of fresh lemon juice
2 canned plum tomatoes, crushed	

Cut the eggplant in half lengthwise. Lightly score each cut side with the tip of a knife in a crosshatch pattern and sprinkle with kosher salt. Place a cake rack on a cookie sheet and place the salted eggplant on the rack, cut side down. Let the eggplant sit for at least 1 hour to let the salt draw out the bitter juices.

Rinse the eggplant and blot it with paper towels. Peel 1 eggplant half and leave the other unpeeled. Cut the eggplant into ½-inch dice.

In a 2½-quart nonreactive saucepan, heat the olive oil over medium heat. Add the garlic and onion and cook, stirring occasionally, until they are soft and a bit browned—about 5 minutes.

Add the eggplant to the pot along with the chicken stock, tomatoes, thyme, oregano, red pepper flakes, and salt. Cook over medium-low heat until the eggplant is thoroughly cooked and soft, about 1 hour.

While the eggplant is simmering, prepare the red bell pepper. Wash it well and place it directly on a stove burner over a high, open flame. If you do not have a gas stove, you can do this under the broiler. Let the pepper become black and charred and rotate it to make sure it cooks evenly. This should take about 20 minutes, depending on the strength of the flame. Remove the pepper from the burner or broiler and wrap it in a kitchen towel. Let it cool for 10 minutes. The peel will now come off the roasted pepper easily; remove the peel by rubbing it off or by dunking the pepper in water.

Remove and discard the stem and seeds from the peeled pepper and place it in a blender.

Take a ladel of the simmering eggplant juice and add it to the pepper. Purée the pepper and set aside.

When the eggplant is done, stir in the roasted red pepper purée and season the dish with a squeeze of lemon. Serve hot.

Yield: 4 servings

Wild Rice Crepes with Apples and Chestnuts

This is a wonderful fall dish. Serve it next to an entrée with a white wine gravy or light cream sauce. Mild garlic, onions, thyme, bay leaf, or sweet spices all would be complementary to the crepes.

A second side dish seems unnecessary—maybe just some simple steamed greens.

1 tart apple, such as Granny Smith	Salt and freshly ground pepper
1 tablespoon unsalted butter	to taste
$\frac{1}{2}$ cup diced onion	Squeeze of fresh lemon juice
$\frac{1}{2}$ cup peeled chestnuts (see Note)	2 Wild Rice Crepes (page 174)

Preheat the oven to 400° F.

Peel and core the apple and cut it into $\frac{1}{2}$-inch cubes.

In a 10-inch skillet, melt the butter over medium heat. Add the onion and sauté, stirring occasionally, for 3 minutes. Add the apple and sauté 5 minutes or until somewhat soft.

Crumble the chestnuts a bit and add them to the pan. Cook another minute, season with salt, pepper, and lemon juice, and remove the mixture to a bowl.

Lay the crepes flat on a work surface with the wild rice side down. Divide the filling between the 2 crepes, arranging it in a strip across the bottom third of the crepe. Fold in the sides and then roll them up.

Place the filled crepes seam side down in a greased pie pan or small baking pan. Cover loosely with foil and bake until hot—about 15 minutes.

Yield: 2 servings

NOTE: Chestnuts may be purchased already peeled, either in cans, frozen or vacuum packed, in any good specialty store.

Spiced Poached Pears in Red Wine

Poached pears are a wonderful accent for game and pork. Their sweetness and acidity can be complementary and palate cleansing. They can be made at least a week ahead of time and stored covered with their poaching liquid. The pears you use for this recipe should be ripe, but not overly so—very ripe pears tend to become mushy when cooked.

The pears work well with many side dishes, but don't pair them with sweet vegetables like turnips, parsnips, or carrots.

2 cups full-bodied red wine, such as Nebbiolo, California Syrah, or Côtes du Rhône	4 whole allspice
	A grating of nutmeg
	10 whole black peppercorns
4 whole cloves	2 bay leaves
1 cinnamon stick	2 ripe pears

Combine the red wine and spices in a deep, nonreactive pot. (If you use a shallow saucepan, you'll need more wine to keep the pears submerged.)

Peel the pears and cut them in half lengthwise. Core them and place them in the pan with the wine. Bring to a boil and then simmer the pears for about 35 minutes. Riper pears will take less time to cook than unripe ones. When done (test by piercing a pear with a toothpick—it should go in easily), gently remove the pears from the liquid. If you are not serving them immediately, let the poaching liquid cool a bit and cover the pears with it.

Yield: 4 servings

NOTE: The pears may be served hot, cold, or at room temperature. They are very pretty when sliced lengthwise, leaving a little bit at the top uncut, and fanned.

Cranberry Compote with Red Wine and Sweet Spices

Fresh cranberry sauce is quite different from the canned variety. Cranberries are incredibly sour, but cooked with sugar and spices, they are transformed into something wonderful and complex.

Cranberry sauce is a must at Thanksgiving, but there is no reason to wait for that holiday to enjoy them. Cranberries are plentiful for a couple of months starting in October, and they can be frozen right in the bag for use year round.

Try serving cranberry sauce with pork, chicken, game birds, or venison.

1 bag cranberries	$\frac{1}{16}$ teaspoon ground ginger
3 tablespoons sugar	A few gratings of nutmeg
1$\frac{1}{3}$ cups full-bodied red wine, such	A few grinds of black pepper
as a Portuguese red, California	1 cinnamon stick
Syrah, or Côtes du Rhône	1-inch strip lemon zest
$\frac{1}{16}$ teaspoon ground cloves	

Look over the cranberries and discard any that are white or withered. Place the remaining cranberries in a heavy-bottomed, nonreactive 2-quart saucepan.

Add the sugar, red wine, cloves, ginger, nutmeg, black pepper, cinnamon stick, and lemon zest. Stir to combine and place the pot over medium heat. Bring the cranberries to a boil, stirring often, and then lower the heat to keep them at a simmer. Continue cooking the cranberries, stirring often and sort of mashing them a bit, until the berries have broken out of their skins and the mixture has become a thick chunky sauce—about 45 minutes. Discard the cinnamon stick.

Taste the sauce—you may want to add more sugar, depending on your preferences. You can serve the sauce immediately or let it cool and serve it at room temperature. I think it is better to make it a few days or even a week ahead and let the flavors meld in the refrigerator.

Yield: 2 cups compote, or 6 to 8 servings

Provençal Tart

This rustic tart relies on the goodness of the ingredients. If truly ripe tomatoes are not available, just leave them out. Serve the tart with lamb or chicken, or perhaps a fish like tuna. All that is needed to round things out is a green salad.

1 recipe whole wheat pie dough
  (page 193)

Olive oil, for brushing and
  drizzling

½ teaspoon minced garlic

1 small onion, peeled and sliced
  ¼ inch thick

1 small eggplant, sliced ¼ inch
  thick

1 small zucchini, sliced ¼ inch
  thick

2 fresh plum tomatoes, seeded and
  sliced ¼ inch thick

Salt and freshly ground pepper to
  taste

1 teaspoon chopped fresh thyme

1 tablespoon grated Parmesan

Preheat the oven to 375° F.

Roll the pie dough out into any shape you like—rectangular, square, or round—leaving it about ⅛ inch thick. Place the rolled dough on a baking sheet and turn the edges up a bit to form a little lip.

Bake the tart shell for 10 to 15 minutes, or until it starts to firm up and is no longer moist on the surface.

Brush the tart shell with a little olive oil and sprinkle with the garlic. Start layering in the vegetables, alternating a slice of onion, then eggplant, then zucchini and tomato so that they overlap a bit. Cover the entire tart shell this way in a single layer.

When all the vegetables are used up, season the tart with salt, pepper, and thyme. Drizzle a bit of olive oil over the whole thing and then sprinkle with the Parmesan. Bake for 35 to 45 minutes, until the crust has browned and the vegetables are cooked.

Yield: 4 to 6 servings

Ratatouille Beggar's Purses

Beggar's purses resemble little tied-up sacks. They are not so much difficult to prepare as they are labor intensive. Although beggar's purses started out as an hors d'oeuvre filled with caviar, they've made their way to the main event here. Ratatouille is a good filling for the crepes because it is soft, malleable, and not too wet, good traits in this instance. Even so, it is not a good idea to fill the crepes too far in advance or they will become soggy.

These purses would be delightful with a lamb dish, whether it is a roast, rack of lamb, or a stew. Chicken, of course, would be augmented happily, as would beef or hearty fish. Try a risotto or rice pilaf with them as well.

4 chives or 1 scallion　　　　　　**1 recipe ratatouille (page 118),**

8 crepes (page 174)　　　　　　　　**warm**

Bring 1 cup of water to a boil in an 8-inch skillet. If using chives, dip them into the water briefly, just enough to make them go limp, but not enough to dull the color. Refresh them under cold water and pat them dry between paper towels. If using scallions, cut off 2 green stalks and then cut each one in half lengthwise. Blanch them in the same way.

Lay a crepe on a work surface, speckled side up. Place about ¼ cup of warm ratatouille in the center and gather up the edges of the crepe to form a pouch. Use a chive or scallion to tie the crepe, knotting it without pulling too tight. Keep the beggar's purse warm in a low-temperature oven while you finish the rest. Repeat with the remaining filling and crepes. Serve immediately.

Yield: 4 servings

Broccoli Strudel

Savory strudels are an amusing and elegant way to accompany a main dish. They look and taste great and are fairly uncomplicated to prepare, yet they score big points in the impressing category. This Broccoli Strudel can be prepared ahead and frozen before baking. It goes right from the freezer into the oven without thawing first—just increase the baking time by 5 or 10 minutes.

You can serve this strudel with any meat or fish, though it would be nice to have a sauce to mingle with the strudel, maybe something with white wine, cream, or mushrooms.

1 head broccoli	¼ teaspoon dried thyme
2 tablespoons olive oil	¼ cup dry bread crumbs
2 tablespoons unsalted butter	⅓ cup grated Parmesan
½ cup diced onion or scallion	Juice of ½ lemon
1 teaspoon minced garlic	Salt and freshly ground pepper
¼ cup white wine	to taste
⅛ teaspoon curry powder	6 sheets phyllo dough, thawed
Small pinch of cayenne pepper	

Trim a couple of inches off the bottom of the broccoli stems and discard. Cut the broccoli into chunks and place them in the bowl of a food processor. Pulse the processor until the broccoli is coarsely chopped; do not overprocess.

Combine the olive oil and butter in a 12-inch skillet and melt over medium-low heat. Pour half into a bowl and reserve for brushing the phyllo. Add the onion or scallion and garlic to the remaining fat in the pan and sweat for about 5 minutes, until soft.

Add the broccoli and white wine to the skillet and cook about 8 minutes, stirring occasionally, until the broccoli has softened a bit and is bright green. Remove from the heat.

Add the curry powder, cayenne, thyme, bread crumbs, Parmesan, lemon juice, salt and pepper and mix thoroughly. Cool to room temperature.

Preheat the oven to 350°F.

Spread a sheet of phyllo on a work surface, with the short edge facing you. Brush lightly with the olive oil–butter mixture. Lay another sheet on top of the first sheet and lightly brush that one, too. Lay a final sheet on top and brush it. Cut the phyllo in half, crosswise. Mound ¼ of the broccoli mixture on the edge of the phyllo nearest you. Roll it up, until you reach the crosswise cut, and place the strudel on a greased sheet pan, seam side down. Continue, using another quarter of the broccoli and the other half of the greased phyllo.

Repeat the process, using the remaining 3 sheets of phyllo and the rest of the broccoli. Brush the tops of the strudel with more of the olive oil–butter mixture and bake for about 25 minutes, until golden brown.

To serve, cut the strudel on the diagonal into 2-inch lengths. Serve the pieces either standing on end or laid flat.

Yield: 8 servings

Herbed Asparagus Timbale

This is a great way to use asparagus stems left over from another recipe that calls only for the tips. It is quite an elegant side dish, suitable for serving with mild fish, chicken, or light game birds. When choosing another side dish to pair with the timbale, look for something crisp and simple to offset the creaminess and delicate flavors of the custard.

1 pound asparagus stems, woody ends removed	**1 teaspoon chopped mixed fresh herbs, such as thyme, chervil, tarragon, parsley**
1¼ cups heavy cream	**¼ teaspoon salt**
1 egg	**Pinch of freshly ground white pepper**
1 egg yolk	

Preheat the oven to 325° F.

Bring 2 quarts of water to a boil. Add the asparagus stems and lower the heat to a simmer. Cook 20 minutes, or until the asparagus is quite tender. Drain and pat very dry.

Purée the asparagus in a food processor or blender until very smooth. For an extra-silky texture, pass the purée through a strainer into a mixing bowl. Let cool to room temperature.

Add the cream, egg, egg yolk, herbs, salt, and pepper to the purée. Whisk well.

Butter 4 ½-cup ramekins very thoroughly. Fill them with the asparagus mixture. Place the ramekins in a roasting pan. Fill the pan with tepid water ⅔ of the way up the sides of the ramekins. Bake for approximately 35 minutes, until the custard has just set. Remove from the water bath and let sit a minute before unmolding. To unmold, run a thin knife around the edge of the custard and invert directly onto a dinner plate.

Yield: 4 servings

Zucchini and Carrot Terrine

Alternating layers of zucchini and carrot purée form a beautiful, colorful terrine. This is another ideal example of how one can take everyday ingredients and transform them into something special. Save this preparation for a sit-down dinner party, when you want a special presentation. You can prepare this terrine a few days ahead of time if you wish.

For a second side dish, choose something to contrast with the creamy texture of the terrine. Either Corn, Red Pepper, and Green Bean Sauté (page 12) or Spaetzle (page 139) would do nicely.

4 zucchini (about 1½ pounds total)	Salt and freshly ground pepper
2 large carrots (about 1 pound)	to taste
6 eggs	A few gratings of nutmeg
1 cup heavy cream	⅛ teaspoon curry powder

Preheat the oven to 350° F.

Trim the ends and cut the zucchini into 2-inch chunks. Trim the ends and peel the carrots and cut them into 2-inch chunks. Place both the zucchini and carrots in a large steamer and steam them for 20 to 25 minutes or until they are soft and cooked all the way through. Test for tenderness with a small knife. Remove the vegetables from the steamer.

When the zucchini is cool enough to handle, squeeze it with your hands to remove as much moisture as you can. Place it in the bowl of a food processor. Add 3 of the eggs and purée 30 seconds. Add ½ cup cream, salt, pepper, nutmeg, and half the curry powder. Continue puréeing until very smooth. Scrape the zucchini mixture into a bowl.

Wash and dry the processor bowl and add the carrots and 3 remaining eggs. Purée 30 seconds. Add the remaining ½ cup heavy cream, salt, pepper, nutmeg, and curry powder. Purée until very smooth. Scrape the carrot mixture into a bowl.

Line a greased 6-cup terrine with parchment paper. With a spatula, spread a ¼-inch layer of carrot purée evenly over the bottom of the terrine. The more neatly you do this the better your finished terrine will look. Carefully spoon a ¼-inch layer of zucchini purée on top of the first layer, smoothing it with the spatula. Alternate layers until you have used all the purée—you'll probably have 4 layers of each. Cover the top with parchment paper.

Place the terrine in a large roasting pan filled halfway with tepid water. Place the pan in the oven and bake for 1½ to 2 hours. The terrine is done when it is just set and feels firm in the middle—be careful not to let it puff up around the edges. If this starts to happen before it is really set, lower the temperature of the oven by 50°. Test the terrine for doneness by inserting a skewer into the center—if it comes out hot and clean, it's done. Remove the terrine from the water bath and let it rest 5 minutes before unmolding.

To unmold, invert the terrine directly onto a work surface. Remove the parchment and then slide the terrine, using a spatula to guide it, onto a serving platter. Alternatively, you can slice the terrine on the work surface and then arrange the slices on a serving platter.

Yield: 8 to 10 servings

NOTE: To reheat, cut ¹/₂-inch slices of the terrine and lay them on a parchment-lined sheet pan. Cover with another piece of parchment and place in a 400°F. oven for 5 to 10 minutes.

Zucchini Blossoms Filled with Lemoned Goat Cheese

This is a beautiful spring or early summer dish that is delicious with lamb or chicken. The blossoms would pair well with Provençal Broiled Tomatoes (page 10), Buttered Zucchini Ribbons (page 81), or julienned carrots and snow peas.

5 ounces soft mild goat cheese, such as Montrachet	**Salt and freshly ground pepper to taste**
¹/₈ teaspoon grated lemon zest	**8 zucchini blossoms**
1 teaspoon fresh lemon juice	

Preheat the oven to 400°F.

In a small bowl, combine the goat cheese, lemon zest, lemon juice, salt, and pepper.

Gently open the blossoms and remove and discard the pistils or stamens. Fill each blossom with the goat cheese mixture and close the ends.

Place the filled blossoms on a greased baking sheet and bake for approximately 10 minutes, until hot. Serve immediately.

Yield: 4 servings

Swiss Chard Tart

Swiss chard is often baked into a tart in France, as a meal in itself. It makes a great side dish, however. Here it is prepared as a large tart to be cut into wedges, but for a more elegant presentation you may prepare individual tarts. Swiss chard has an earthy green flavor that might overwhelm some mild-tasting fish, but otherwise it can be served with a wide range of entrées. Avoid rich cream sauces, as the tart is itself quite rich. Try it with meats prepared with Provençale flavorings such as olives, tomatoes, onions, and garlic. It would be especially nice next to a roast duck.

1 recipe chilled Tart Pastry
    (page 192), left at room
    temperature for 15 minutes
¾ pound Swiss chard
1 tablespoon unsalted butter
1 small onion, thinly sliced
1 large garlic clove, minced
Salt and freshly ground pepper
    to taste

1 cup heavy cream
2 eggs
1 egg yolk
A grating of nutmeg
Pinch of cayenne pepper
2 tablespoons grated Parmesan
    (optional)

Lightly dust a flat surface with flour and roll out the pastry to fit a 10-inch tart pan. Line the pan with the dough, crimping the edges. Refrigerate the tart shell for 1 hour.

Preheat the oven to 375° F.

Remove the shell from the refrigerator and line it with foil. Fill the shell with uncooked dried beans or pie weights and bake it for about 15 minutes. Remove the foil and beans or pie weights and continue baking the shell another 5 minutes. Remove the shell from the oven and let it cool a bit. Reduce the oven temperature to 350° F.

While the shell is baking, prepare the filling. Trim the Swiss chard of any brown edges. Coarsely chop it at ½-inch intervals.

Melt the butter in a 10-inch sauté pan over medium-low heat. Add the onion and sweat it for about 5 minutes, until translucent and soft. Add the garlic and sweat another minute. Add the chard and cook, tossing occasionally until the chard is wilted, about 10 minutes. Season lightly with salt and pepper, then cool to room temperature.

In a mixing bowl, whisk together the cream, eggs, egg yolk, nutmeg, and cayenne.

Fill the prebaked tart shell with the Swiss chard mixture. Pour the custard over the filling and gently stir a bit to blend. Sprinkle with Parmesan if you like and bake for 35 to 40 minutes, until set and lightly browned. Serve immediately or at room temperature.

Yield: 8 servings

NOTE: This will keep several days and can be reheated in a 350°F. oven for 15 minutes.

Ramps with Mushrooms and Egg Noodles

Ramps, otherwise known as wild leeks, are a dark green, pungently flavored vegetable. Nothing can compare with their deep, seductive taste. They are a sign of spring, along with shad roe, fiddlehead ferns, and soft-shelled crabs, and each year I look forward to them almost as eagerly as to my first crab sandwich!

If ramps are unavailable, try this recipe with spinach. Serve it with roast chicken, steaks, or veal.

2 cups ½-inch-wide uncooked egg noodles	2 tablespoons unsalted butter
½ pound ramps, well washed	Small pinch of grated nutmeg
2 teaspoons olive oil	Salt and freshly ground pepper to taste
8 large button mushrooms, sliced	

Cook the egg noodles in boiling salted water until al dente. Drain, rinse, and set aside.

Clean the ramps by trimming the root end. Cut the ramps into 2-inch lengths, including the slender stalk, and set aside.

In a 12-inch sauté pan, heat the olive oil over high heat until smoking. Add the sliced mushrooms and sauté, tossing, until they are browned, 3 to 5 minutes.

Reduce the heat to medium and add the butter to the sauté pan. When it is melted, add the ramps and cooked egg noodles. Season with the grated nutmeg, salt, and pepper and cook, stirring, until the ramps have just wilted. Serve immediately.

Yield: 4 servings

Tomato Risotto

Much has been written about risotto, that comforting rice dish from Italy, so I won't add to all the fuss. This version, tinted pink from tomato, would be lovely with almost any meat or fish, or as part of an elegant vegetarian meal, although I don't think that risotto should be limited to fancier meals. It is the kind of side dish that transforms a simple grilled chop into something special.

Once you've learned the technique for preparing risotto, you can vary the flavoring to suit your entrée and mood (and pocketbook), using everything from squid to truffles. Just be sure to use the squat Arborio rice to ensure the proper texture.

Pair this with Sautéed Escarole with Garlic and Lemon (page 25) or Sautéed Mushrooms with Oregano (page 8).

1 tablespoon olive oil	½ cup tomato sauce
1 teaspoon minced garlic	1 tablespoon unsalted butter
½ cup diced onion	Salt and freshly ground pepper
2 cups uncooked Arborio rice	to taste
4 cups hot chicken stock	Grated Parmesan
1 cup white wine	Chopped parsley

In a 3-quart heavy-bottomed sauce pot, heat the olive oil over medium heat. Add the garlic and onion and gently sauté them, stirring often, until translucent, about 5 minutes.

Add the rice and sauté, stirring, until it is translucent, about 3 minutes. Be careful that it doesn't brown.

Add ½ cup of hot chicken stock, stirring. Adjust the heat so that the stock simmers a bit as you stir it and continue stirring until the stock is absorbed. Add another ½ cup of hot stock and continue to stir. Repeat, using ½ cup of stock at a time, never ceasing to stir, until you have used about half the stock. At this point, add ½ cup of the wine, stir until it is absorbed, and then add the next ½ cup of wine. Finish adding the stock as before, tasting the risotto toward the end to check for doneness—it should be creamy, but each grain should have a firm center. When it is done to your liking, take the risotto off the heat, stir in the tomato sauce, butter, salt, and pepper.

Serve the risotto in a serving bowl, sprinkled generously with Parmesan and parsley.

Yield: 4 to 6 servings

NOTE: You can prepare the risotto until almost done, using 3½ cups of the stock, and leave it on the burner with the heat off for a half hour or so. It will firm up quickly, but when you are ready to serve, turn the heat back on and add the remaining ½ cup of stock. The risotto will loosen up as you stir and you can finish it as described in the recipe.

Creamy Rice with Feta

This rice dish is a must with leg of lamb or broiled lamb chops. It also pairs well with some fish— panfried flounder or skate, for example. It's also a great way to use leftover rice. Serve it in combination with simple green beans, asparagus, or broccoli.

¾ **cup uncooked white rice**	¼ **cup fresh feta cheese, crumbled**
1¼ **cups water**	**Squeeze of fresh lemon juice**
2 **teaspoons olive oil**	**Salt and freshly ground pepper**
1 **tablespoon minced shallot**	**to taste**
½ **cup heavy cream**	

Place the rice and water in a 1-quart saucepan. Bring to a boil over high heat, lower the heat as much as you can, and cover the pot. Cook exactly 20 minutes. Uncover and fluff the rice with a fork.

In a 10-inch sauté pan, heat the olive oil over medium heat. Add the shallot and gently sauté until translucent, but not browned, about 2 minutes.

Add the cream and feta, raise the heat to high, and bring to a boil. Continue boiling for 1 minute or until the mixture thickens somewhat.

Lower the heat to medium, add the rice, and heat it thoroughly, stirring constantly.

Season to taste with the lemon juice, salt, and pepper.

Yield: 2 to 4 servings

NOTE: Feta is a pressed and brined cheese most commonly associated with Greek cuisine. Very good Hungarian, Bulgarian, French, Israeli, and Turkish feta can also be found.

Saffron Pilaf with Almonds and Raisins

The seasonings in this pilaf give it a Middle Eastern character, bringing to mind lamb stew or kebabs, curried chicken or pork. Of course, it's also good for brightening up a plain roast. You can prepare the pilaf with everyday long-grain rice, but for something extra special try using aromatic basmati rice. Pair it with Buttered Zucchini Ribbons (page 81), Chickpea Stew with Middle Eastern Spices (page 131), or Spicy Gingered Carrots (page 22).

1 tablespoon unsalted butter	½ cup raisins or currants
½ cup diced onion	½ cup sliced almonds
2 cups uncooked white rice	Salt to taste
3 cups chicken stock	1 tablespoon chopped fresh parsley
1 teaspoon saffron	

Preheat the oven to 350° F.

Melt the butter in an ovenproof casserole over medium-low heat. Add the onion and sweat, stirring occasionally, until the onion is translucent, about 5 minutes. Lower the heat if it starts to brown.

Add the rice and cook, stirring, until it turns somewhat opaque, about 2 minutes. Be careful not to brown the rice.

Add the chicken stock and saffron and stir well. Raise the heat to high and bring to a boil, stirring occasionally. Remove from the heat, cover, and place in the oven for 10 minutes.

Add the raisins or currants to the rice without stirring, re-cover, and continue baking for another 10 minutes or until the liquid is absorbed. Uncover the rice, stir half the almonds into the rice with a bit of salt, and then sprinkle the remaining almonds on top. Garnish with the chopped parsley and serve immediately.

Yield: 6 to 8 servings

Curried Couscous with Pine Nuts and Currants

This dish is great with grilled or roast chicken, pork, or lamb, as well as stews seasoned with Middle Eastern spices. Try it also with some grilled vegetables brushed with olive oil for a vegetarian meal. It works well in combination with spinach with lemon and garlic or Buttered Zucchini Ribbons (page 81); the green of both sets off the yellow couscous beautifully.

2½ cups uncooked couscous	2 tablespoons fresh lemon juice
1 tablespoon olive oil	1 teaspoon salt
1 cup very hot water	6 dashes Tabasco
½ cup (1 stick) unsalted butter	½ cup toasted pine nuts
½ cup minced onion	½ cup currants
3½ tablespoons Madras-style curry powder	

Place the couscous in a bowl. Add the olive oil and rub the couscous with your hands to thoroughly coat each grain with the oil. Add the hot water and stir well until the water is absorbed.

In a 10-inch sauté pan, melt the butter over medium-low heat. Add the onion and cook gently until it is soft, about 10 minutes.

Add the curry powder and cook another 2 minutes, stirring. Be sure you do not brown the curry powder or it will become bitter.

Add the couscous, lemon juice, salt, Tabasco, pine nuts, and currants. Stir well to distribute the seasonings. Cook until the couscous is hot, and serve.

Yield: 4 to 6 servings

NOTE: If you mince the onion while the couscous is steaming, you can keep the time required for this recipe to under half an hour. This can be made up to a week ahead of time and reheated, covered, in a 350° F. oven for about 15 minutes.

Mushroom Ravioli

Ravioli make a fun yet elegant side dish. You can vary the filling as you wish, tailoring it to complement your entrée. These mushroom ravioli are well suited to a wide selection of main courses: chicken, beef, pork, veal, game birds, and most fish. A sauce is quite desirable, and many flavors would work with the ravioli: garlic, herbs, wine, olives, and lemon, to name a few.

You may freeze the filling and / or the dough separately if you wish. You can also complete the ravioli without boiling them and then freeze them. To cook, drop the ravioli into boiling salted water while still frozen—do not thaw first or they will become sticky.

2 10-ounce boxes cultivated button mushrooms	1 teaspoon dried thyme
2 shallots, peeled and quartered	1 teaspoon dried sage
2 tablespoons unsalted butter, softened	Dash of brandy, Madeira, or port
	Salt and freshly ground pepper to taste
¼ cup fresh bread crumbs	1 recipe Basic Pasta Dough
¼ cup grated Parmesan	All-purpose flour, for dusting
Juice of ½ lemon	1 egg, beaten

Wipe the mushrooms clean with a damp paper towel. Cut each one in half or in quarters, depending on its size. Place the mushrooms and shallots in the bowl of a food processor and pulse them until they are finely chopped.

In a 10-inch sauté pan, melt 1 tablespoon of the butter over medium-low heat. Add the mushroom mixture and cook slowly, stirring occasionally, until the mushroom liquid has rendered and evaporated, about 25 minutes.

Remove the mushrooms to a mixing bowl and add the remaining butter, bread crumbs, Parmesan, lemon juice, thyme, sage, brandy, salt, and pepper. Mix well, and adjust the seasonings. Let cool.

Roll out 6 thin sheets of pasta dough, according to the directions for your machine. Lightly dust them with flour as they are done and keep them covered with plastic wrap or a towel until ready to use.

Lightly dust a ravioli mold with flour. Lay 1 sheet of dough on top of it and use the plastic mold provided to make indentations. With a pastry brush, lightly but thoroughly brush egg wash along the borders of each ravioli.

Fill each ravioli with the mushroom mixture. Lay the second sheet of pasta on top and press gently with your palms to push out any air and seal lightly. Using a rolling pin, seal and cut out the ravioli by rolling on top of the mold. Turn over the mold to release the ravioli. Repeat with the remaining sheets of pasta or until all the filling is used.

Drop the ravioli into 4 quarts of boiling salted water and cook for 2 to 3 minutes, until just cooked. Drain well and serve.

Yield: 3 dozen ravioli

NOTE: If not serving immediately, drain the ravioli well and toss with a little olive oil to prevent them from sticking together. To reheat, immerse them briefly in boiling water or quickly sauté in olive oil until lightly browned.

Basic Pasta Dough

This dough may be made a day or two ahead of time and kept in the refrigerator, well wrapped. It may also be frozen; just thaw in the refrigerator.

2 cups unbleached all-purpose flour	**1 tablespoon olive oil**
2 eggs	**Pinch of kosher salt**
2 tablespoons water	

Place the flour in a mixing bowl and make a well in the center.

In a small bowl, lightly whisk together the eggs, water, olive oil, and salt. Pour them into the well in the flour.

Using a fork, stir the liquids in a circular motion, slowly incorporating the flour. Use your hands when the dough becomes too stiff.

Turn the dough out onto a floured board and knead it until it becomes smooth and elastic, about 10 minutes. Cover in plastic and let rest, refrigerated, for at least 1 hour before using.

Yield: makes approximately 3 dozen ravioli

Ratatouille Ravioli

This recipe makes more than enough filling for 4 servings of ravioli, but since ratatouille takes time to prepare, you might as well make plenty. It keeps well, and, besides, it's almost impossible to make just a little. Either triple the pasta recipe and use all the ratatouille for ravioli and freeze what you don't need immediately, use it to fill Beggar's Purses (page 105), or just serve the ratatouille by itself as a side dish another day.

These ravioli go great with many full-flavored meat dishes and some of the heartier fish. Think of serving them with beef stew, lamb, roast chicken with garlic, or barbecued swordfish or tuna.

2 tablespoons olive oil	2 teaspoons dried oregano
1 small onion, peeled, cut in half, and sliced	1 sprig fresh rosemary
3 garlic cloves, minced	1 bay leaf
1 smallish eggplant, cut in ¼-inch dice	Juice of ½ lemon
1 large zucchini, cut in ¼-inch dice	Salt and freshly ground pepper to taste
1 anchovy	
1 cup canned crushed tomatoes	½ recipe Basic Pasta Dough (page 117)
1 teaspoon dried thyme or 1 large sprig fresh thyme	All-purpose flour, for dusting
	1 egg, beaten

Heat the olive oil over medium heat in a 12-inch skillet. Add the onion and garlic and sauté, stirring, for about 2 minutes, until they are soft but not browned.

Add the eggplant, zucchini, anchovy, tomatoes, and herbs and stir to combine. Cook over medium-low heat for a half hour, just enough to soften but not brown the vegetables.

Cover the ratatouille and cook for another half hour, stirring occasionally, until the vegetables are quite soft. Season with the lemon juice, salt, and pepper.

Remove the ratatouille from the skillet and set aside to cool.

Roll out 2 thin sheets of pasta dough, according to the directions for your machine. Lightly dust the sheets with flour and keep them covered with plastic wrap or a towel until ready to use.

Lightly dust a ravioli mold with flour. Lay 1 sheet of dough on top of it and use the plastic mold provided to make indentations. With a pastry brush, lightly but thoroughly brush egg wash along the borders of each ravioli.

Fill each ravioli with the ratatouille. Lay the second sheet of pasta on top and press gently with your palms to push out any air and seal lightly. Using a rolling pin, seal and cut out the ravioli by rolling firmly over the mold. Turn the mold over to release the ravioli.

Drop the ravioli into 4 quarts of boiling salted water and cook for 2 to 3 minutes, until just cooked. Drain well and serve.

Yield: 1 dozen ravioli

NOTE: If not serving immediately, drain the ravioli well and toss with a little olive oil to prevent them from sticking together. To reheat, immerse them briefly in boiling water or quickly sauté in olive oil until lightly browned.

Homey Sides

Every nation has its own distinctive comfort foods. These are the hearty dishes prepared by families in their homes and in restaurants catering to those looking for a "home-style" meal. Homey sides are generally uncomplicated and may evoke memories of our childhoods—big bowls of steaming mashed potatoes, endless quantities of creamed corn, dollops of applesauce to eat with our pork chops, or seductively crisp hash browns made with leftover potatoes. Homey sides evoke plenitude, generosity, and goodness. They can completely change the tone of a meal and are often met with an enthusiastic "ooh" and "oh boy!"

Certain meals are just not complete without a homey side. Smoked ham would be lonely without its collards, and roast beef would pine for a friendly bowl of mashed potatoes and gravy or a skillet full of hash. Homey foods make up many of our classic dinner combinations and should not be overlooked.

Applesauce ◆ *Cabbage Rolls with Zucchini and Tomato* ◆ *Cabbage Rolls with Mushrooms and Barley* ◆ *Kale with Bacon and Onion* ◆ *Southern Collard Greens* ◆ *Creamed Spinach* ◆ *How to Steam Spinach* ◆ *Sautéed Barley with Duck Fat and Kale* ◆ *Chickpea Stew with Middle Eastern Spices* ◆ *Haricots Blanc, Gascon Style* ◆ *BBQ Baked Beans* ◆ *Black Beans with Ham Hock* ◆ *Lentil Stew with Tomato* ◆ *Cheese Grits* ◆ *The Best Creamed Corn* ◆ *Succotash* ◆ *Spaetzle* ◆ *Sweet Potato Hash with Pecans* ◆ *Mashed Potatoes with Roasted Garlic and Garlic Chips* ◆ *Potato Tots* ◆ *Cumin-Glazed Sweet Potatoes* ◆ *Potato Hash with Mushrooms* ◆ *My Grandmother's Orzo*

Applesauce

Applesauce is the perfect accompaniment for pork chops, as well as all kinds of sausages and wursts. Sometimes I just have a little applesauce left over and a little cranberry compote (page 103), and I mix them together. Choose a green vegetable and Potato Cake with Scallion (page 70) to go alongside.

8 apples, such as Cortland	**1 whole clove**
½ cup apple cider or water	**Salt and freshly ground pepper**
Small pinch of cinnamon	**to taste**

Peel and core the apples and cut them into chunks. Place the apples in a nonreactive 2-quart saucepan along with the cider or water, cinnamon, clove, salt, and pepper.

Cover the pot and cook over medium-low heat for about 10 minutes. Remove the cover and stir well. Continue cooking uncovered, stirring occasionally, until the apples have thickened into a sauce, about another 30 minutes. Discard the clove. Serve hot or cold.

Yield: 2 cups

NOTE: This keeps for a month in the refrigerator.

Cabbage Rolls with Zucchini and Tomato

These rolls would be best served with pork or hearty fish, or perhaps chicken or guinea hen. With them I would serve Potato Cake with Scallion (page 70) or perhaps Saffron Pilaf with Almonds and Raisins (page 114).

2 teaspoons olive oil	Pinch of dried thyme
½ teaspoon minced garlic	2 tablespoons white wine
⅓ cup diced onion	Salt and freshly ground pepper
1 medium zucchini, cut into	to taste
½-inch dice (about 1 cup)	6 large cabbage leaves
3 fresh plum tomatoes, seeded and	½ cup chicken stock
cut into ½-inch dice	

In a small saucepan, heat the olive oil over medium-low heat. Add the garlic and onion and cook, stirring occasionally, for 5 minutes or until softened.

Add the zucchini, tomatoes, thyme, wine, salt, and pepper. Cook over medium-low heat for about 20 minutes, until the vegetables have softened and the wine has evaporated. Taste and adjust the seasonings.

While the zucchini mixture is cooking, steam the cabbage leaves or blanch them in boiling salted water until they are soft and flexible. Trim the tough center stems to make them thinner and more flexible and pat the leaves dry. (The recipe can be prepared ahead to this point.)

Preheat the oven to 350° F.

Divide the zucchini filling between the cabbage leaves and roll up, tucking in the ends as you go. Place the rolls in a baking pan just large enough to hold them without crowding. Pour the stock over the rolls, cover the pan with foil, and bake until hot—how long this takes depends on how hot the filling was to begin with. It will take about 35 minutes if everything was cold. Serve immediately.

Yield: 6 rolls

Cabbage Rolls with Mushrooms and Barley

These are a wonderful way to use up leftover barley, but are worthwhile even if the barley must be cooked from scratch. They have an earthy, nonaggressive character that makes them very versatile. Serve them with chicken or game, hearty fish, pork, or beef.

Turnip Purée with Garlic Butter (page 42) or Buttered Zucchini Ribbons (page 81) would be fine partners.

1 tablespoon unsalted butter or rendered chicken or duck fat	8 good-sized cabbage leaves
½ cup diced onion	1 cup cooked barley
2 cups sliced mushrooms	Salt and freshly ground pepper to taste

Melt the butter or fat in a 10-inch skillet over medium heat. Add the onion and sauté, stirring occasionally, until it is softened and somewhat browned—5 to 8 minutes.

Add the mushrooms and cook, stirring occasionally, until they are browned—about 10 minutes.

While the onion and mushrooms are cooking, prepare the cabbage leaves. Trim the hard center vein and then steam the leaves or blanch them in boiling salted water until they are soft—about 5 minutes.

When the mushrooms are cooked, add the barley, salt, and pepper and stir to combine. Cook until heated through.

As soon as the cabbage leaves are cool enough to handle, place about 3 tablespoons of the hot barley mixture in the center of each leaf and roll up like an eggroll. If you find it too difficult to work with the hot leaves, wait until they are a bit cooler, roll with the barley mixture, and then give them a few minutes in a hot oven.

Yield: 8 rolls

NOTE: Both the cabbage and barley can be prepared a couple of days in advance. The rolls can then be heated, covered, in a 375°F. oven for about 20 minutes.

Kale with Bacon and Onion

Kale is a much underappreciated green, but I love it for its sturdy texture and the intense green of both its color and flavor. You can serve this dish with many entrées, but I would stay away from overly delicate preparations. As an accompanying side dish, try Parmesan Spoonbread (page 171) or a potato or turnip gratin.

4 ¼-inch-thick strips slab bacon, cut crosswise into ½-inch pieces	Salt and freshly ground pepper to taste
1 small onion	1 tablespoon white wine vinegar
4 cups roughly chopped kale	

In a 10-inch sauté pan, slowly cook the bacon over medium-low heat to render the fat and crisp the meat, about 10 minutes.

While the bacon is cooking, prepare the onion. Cut off both ends and then cut it in half lengthwise. Peel the onion and then slice it lengthwise, producing half-moons.

When the bacon is pretty crisp, but not too crisp, add the onion slices to the pan and sauté them in the bacon fat until they are softened, about 3 minutes.

Raise the heat to high, add the kale, salt, and pepper and sauté, tossing until the kale is hot and somewhat wilted. (Because of its sturdiness, it won't wilt like spinach—you want it to retain its integrity.) Season with the vinegar and serve immediately.

Yield: 4 servings

Southern Collard Greens

Collard greens are a mainstay of southern American cuisine. They are served with meat and fish, whether it be roasted, smothered, fried, or barbecued. Those of you being initiated to greens here might be pleasantly surprised by them and wonder where they've been all your life.

Serve them with other southern-style sides, like Cheese Grits (page 136), Basic Biscuits (page 176), Bacon Cornsticks (page 175), Parmesan Spoonbread (page 171), or Hush Puppies (page 67).

Collards have tough leaves and are frequently long-simmered to render them more tender, although this is not really necessary. The 2-hour cooking time given here still results in a pleasantly toothsome green—many people cook them even longer than that.

3 strips slab bacon	Salt and freshly ground pepper to
2 big bunches collard greens	taste
(1½ to 2 pounds)	Squeeze of fresh lemon juice or
2 scallions, sliced	1 teaspoon white vinegar

Cut the bacon crosswise into ½-inch pieces. Cook the bacon over medium-low heat in a 4-quart, heavy-bottomed saucepan until the fat is rendered and the bacon is crisp.

While the bacon is cooking, prepare the greens. Cut off and discard about 4 inches of stem. Roughly chop the remaining greens, chopping the stems more than the leaves. Wash thoroughly.

Add the greens to the pot along with the scallions and a cup of water. Cover and cook over medium-low heat. Check the greens from time to time, stir them up, and add more water if it has evaporated. Cook them for about 2 hours, until the greens are softened and dark.

Season with salt, pepper, and lemon or vinegar.

Yield: 4 to 6 servings

Creamed Spinach

This has got to be one of the most beloved sides ever devised. It's a classic at Thanksgiving dinners, but by no means should it be limited to that one day. It's great with all sorts of poultry dishes, beef, veal, pork, shellfish, and shrimp. Serve Creamed Spinach with Tomatoes Stuffed with Basmati Rice (page 9), Potato Tots (page 142), or Braised Leeks (page 20).

Fresh spinach is preferred for this dish, but I've made it lots of times with frozen spinach and never had a complaint! It will keep for quite a while in the refrigerator.

2 bunches fresh spinach (about 2 pounds) or 1 10-ounce package frozen spinach, thawed	**⅛ teaspoon dried thyme**
	A few gratings of nutmeg
	Small pinch of cayenne pepper
1 teaspoon unsalted butter	**Salt to taste**
1 teaspoon minced garlic	**3 grinds of black pepper**
¾ cup Béchamel Sauce (page 191)	**Squeeze of fresh lemon juice**

Remove and discard the tough stems from the spinach leaves and wash the leaves thoroughly. Place the spinach in a large pot and, over medium-low heat, steam the spinach with only the water clinging to its leaves until just wilted. Drain, and when cool enough to handle, squeeze out the liquid. If using frozen spinach, just squeeze out as much water as you can. Roughly chop the spinach.

In a 2-quart heavy-bottomed, nonreactive saucepan, melt the butter over medium heat. Add the garlic and cook until fragrant, about 1 minute, being careful not to let it brown.

Add the chopped spinach to the pot, along with the béchamel, thyme, nutmeg, cayenne, salt, and pepper. Cook over low heat, stirring, until the béchamel is fluid. Continue cooking, keeping the creamed spinach at a very gentle simmer and stirring often, for 30 minutes or until the spinach is very soft.

Season with the lemon juice and adjust the seasonings. Serve at once or let cool and refrigerate.

Yield: 2 to 4 servings

How to Steam Spinach

Perfectly steamed and verdant spinach is easy and quick to achieve. First, wash the spinach well. Drain it, but don't dry it. Then place it in a pot and do not add any water beyond what is left clinging to the leaves. You can add a lump of butter as the spinach cooks if you wish. The pot doesn't even have to be big enough to hold all the spinach at once—you can add more as it wilts. To retain the bright green color of spinach or any other green vegetable, never cover the pot. Cook the spinach over medium heat, stirring it every minute or so to get the unwilted leaves to the bottom. Spinach is delicate and will cook quickly. Cook it just long enough to wilt it, as further cooking will ruin the color. Take the cooked spinach out of the pot with tongs, letting the excess moisture drip back into the pot. Season with salt, pepper, and a little squeeze of lemon if you like, and serve.

This method works well for hardier greens, too, like kale, mustard greens, or Swiss chard. For those larger leaves I usually use a 10-inch sauté pan, add a bit of butter, salt, and the greens, and cook as described above. For particularly rugged greens like kale or collards, add about $\frac{1}{4}$ cup of water.

Sautéed Barley with Duck Fat and Kale

I love this dish with any kind of poultry or game. Sometimes I have it for breakfast with fried or poached eggs. As an accompanying side dish, mushroom preparations are a natural, but Winter Vegetable Purée with Sweet Spices and Crispy Shallots (page 40) or Turnip Gratin (page 40), would also work well.

Duck fat lends a particularly desirable flavor to the dish, but you can substitute rendered bacon fat or olive oil. You can use leftover Barley Pilaf (page 84) or plain boiled barley for this recipe.

1 tablespoon rendered duck fat	**2 cups cooked barley**
2 tablespoons chopped onion	**Salt and freshly ground pepper**
1½ cups coarsely chopped kale	**to taste**

In a 10-inch skillet, melt the duck fat over medium-high heat. Add the onion and sauté, tossing, until the onion has begun to brown somewhat—about 3 minutes.

Add the kale and sauté, tossing, until the kale has wilted a little—about 1 minute.

Add the barley, salt, and pepper and toss together until heated through.

Yield: 2 servings

Chickpea Stew with Middle Eastern Spices

These highly seasoned chickpeas would go particularly well with pork or lamb, as well as fish like tuna or swordfish. Serve them with some steamed spinach or Saffron Pilaf with Almonds and Raisins (page 114).

This stew keeps very well in the refrigerator and is also good at room temperature with some pita bread.

2 cups cooked or canned chickpeas

1 cup chicken stock

¼ cup chopped onion

2 ⅛-inch-thick slices fresh ginger

⅛ teaspoon cayenne pepper

1 teaspoon ground cumin

½ teaspoon ground coriander

¼ teaspoon saffron

Salt to taste

1 fresh plum tomato, seeded and
    diced, or 1 canned plum tomato,
    crushed

Squeeze of fresh lemon juice

In a 2-quart saucepan combine the chickpeas, stock, onion, ginger, cayenne, cumin, coriander, saffron, and salt. Bring to a boil and then gently cook, uncovered, over low heat, stirring occasionally, until the stew has thickened a bit—about 15 minutes. You may have to add a little more stock as it cooks.

Add the tomato and cook another 2 minutes, until it is softened. Add a squeeze of lemon juice and adjust the seasonings.

Yield: 2 to 4 servings

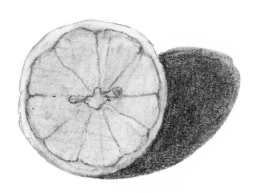

Haricots Blanc, Gascon Style

This peasant bean dish is a mainstay of southwestern France, often used in combination with pre-served duck or goose. It would also be great with a pork roast, chicken, sausages, or ham. While the preparation time is lengthy, once the beans are going they do not require any more attention than an occasional stir. For a more authentic version, use duck or goose fat instead of olive oil.

1 pound dried white beans, preferably Great Northern	1 quart chicken stock
2 tablespoons olive oil	1 cup canned crushed tomatoes
1 medium carrot, peeled and finely chopped	1 teaspoon dried thyme
1 large onion, finely chopped	2 bay leaves
5 garlic cloves, finely chopped	Salt and freshly ground pepper to taste

Bring the beans to a boil in 1 quart of salted water. Remove from the heat and let them soak for 1 hour. Drain.

In a heavy-bottomed pot, heat the olive oil over medium heat. Add the carrot, onion, and garlic and sauté lightly, stirring, until the onion is translucent, 3 or 4 minutes.

Add the beans, chicken stock, tomatoes, thyme, and bay leaves. Stir to combine well. Raise the heat and bring to a boil. Lower the heat to very low and slowly simmer the beans for about 2½ hours, stirring occasionally, until they are soft and have begun to get creamy. Add more stock or water as necessary to keep the beans covered. Season with the salt and pepper. Serve hot.

Yield: 8 servings

NOTE: These beans keep very well in the refrigerator. They might need a little extra water when being reheated. Reheat over low heat on top of the stove. Alternatively, try placing the beans in a casserole, sprinkle the top with bread crumbs and olive oil, and bake at 350° F. for about 30 minutes, until bubbling.

BBQ Baked Beans

Baked beans are a great side dish and one that can be made at any time to keep on hand in the refrigerator. Once you learn the process, you can vary the ingredients as you wish, using more or less of different sweeteners, spices, and seasonings. The small navy bean is most often used for baked beans, but you can really use any dried bean you want.

Serve baked beans with hot dogs and hamburgers, chicken, or pork. Panfried fish would work well, too. Potato Salad, Picnic Style (page 162), Backyard Coleslaw (page 153), Southern Collard Greens (page 128), or Cheese Grits (page 136) all make fun accompaniments.

½ pound dried navy beans	2 tablespoons cider vinegar
½ cup molasses	2 teaspoons chili powder
3 tablespoons ketchup	2 to 3 cups water
1 tablespoon Dijon mustard	Salt to taste
1½ teaspoons minced garlic	1 2-inch-by-2-inch piece slab
1 medium onion, peeled and diced	bacon
¼ teaspoon cayenne pepper	

In a 3-quart saucepan combine the beans with 6 cups of water and bring to a boil over high heat. Lower the heat and simmer for 2 to 2½ hours, stirring occasionally, until the beans are tender. Drain.

Preheat the oven to 325°F.

Combine the cooked beans, molasses, ketchup, mustard, garlic, onion, cayenne, vinegar, chili powder, 2 cups water, salt, and bacon in an 8-cup casserole. Stir to combine and cover with foil.

Bake the beans for 3½ to 4 hours, stirring every once in a while, until the beans are very tender and the liquid has thickened. If the baked beans get too dry during cooking, just stir in some more water; if they are too soupy, remove the foil during the last 45 minutes of cooking. It's hard to be exact with beans; you've just got to use your judgment. When they are done, remove them from the oven and serve immediately or let them cool and refrigerate them. They can be reheated right in the casserole or in smaller batches, with a little extra water, in a skillet.

Yield: 4 to 6 servings

Black Beans with Ham Hock

I must confess that I usually serve these beans as the main part of a meal, with rice and perhaps fried plantain. They do, however, make a great and filling side dish, comforting in cold weather. They work nicely as part of a buffet or as an accompaniment to any uncomplicated, robust entrée.

1 smoked ham hock	1 teaspoon dried thyme
4 cups chicken stock	2 bay leaves
1 tablespoon olive oil	¼ teaspoon hot red pepper flakes
2 teaspoons minced garlic	2 teaspoons sherry vinegar
1 small onion, peeled and diced	A few grinds of black pepper
6 cups black beans, soaked overnight in water to cover	

In a 3½-quart saucepan, cover the ham hock with the stock. Bring to a boil and then simmer, uncovered, for 1 hour. You may have to add water to keep the hock covered. Remove from the heat and reserve.

In another 3½-quart saucepan, heat the olive oil over medium heat. Add the garlic and onion and sauté lightly for about 5 minutes, until softened but not browned.

Drain the black beans from their soaking liquid and add them to the pot. Cover them with the ham hock liquid and add the hock, thyme, bay leaves, and red pepper flakes. Add more stock or water if necessary to cover the beans. Bring the beans to a boil, stirring occasionally to keep them from sticking. Lower the heat and simmer for about 1 hour and 35 minutes, stirring occasionally and adding more liquid if necessary. The beans should be thoroughly cooked and become a nice stew with a silky consistency.

Remove the bay leaf and ham hock from the beans; discard the bay leaf. When the ham hock is cool enough to handle, cut the meat off the bones, shred or chop it, and return it to the beans. Season the beans with the sherry vinegar and black pepper. Serve hot.

Yield: 8 to 10 servings

NOTE: The flavor of the beans improves with age. Leftovers may be reheated or turned into Mashed Black Bean Cakes with Cilantro (page 66).

Lentil Stew with Tomato

Unlike most dried legumes, lentils take only forty minutes or so to cook. This is a substantial side dish that is easily made and keeps well in the refrigerator. Serve it with some greens or rice.

1 tablespoon olive oil	½ teaspoon dried oregano
1 small onion, peeled and diced	1 teaspoon dried thyme
2 garlic cloves, finely chopped	⅛ teaspoon hot red pepper flakes
1 small carrot, peeled and diced	1 bay leaf
1½ cups dried brown lentils	Salt and freshly ground pepper
4 cups chicken stock	to taste
1 cup canned crushed tomatoes	
½ cup red wine, such as a Côtes du	
Rhône or California Syrah	

In a heavy nonreactive saucepan, heat the olive oil over medium heat. Add the onion, garlic, and carrot and sauté gently for 5 minutes, until the vegetables are softened.

Add the lentils, stock, tomatoes, red wine, oregano, thyme, red pepper flakes, and bay leaf. Bring to a boil over high heat and then lower the heat and simmer very gently for about 1 hour, until the lentils are tender. You may have to add a bit more liquid to keep the lentils from getting too dry, but the liquid should reduce and thicken to a nice sauce.

Discard the bay leaf and season with the salt and pepper. Serve hot.

Yield: 6 servings

Cheese Grits

Grits are ground hominy, which is corn that has been treated with lye to puff it and remove the hull. Grits are, of course, quite popular in our southern states, where they are often served at breakfast. You might categorize grits as American polenta, except that they are white. Inexpensive and satisfying, grits can be prepared in any number of ways. You can use water or stock for the liquid; make them soupy or thick; add cheese, herbs, or hot sauce; serve them with eggs, with sausages or with bacon crumbled on top, with breakfast beefsteak or ham; or eat a bowl on their own. You can eat them in the fluid state or let them set up, then cut them into shapes and panfry them. They make a wonderful side dish when you are looking for a homey American touch.

Serve them with other side dishes reminiscent of the South, like collard greens (page 128), sweet potatoes, and black-eyed peas, as well as pickled onion salad and relishes.

3 cups water or chicken stock	**1 cup grated sharp cheese, such as**
1 teaspoon salt	**Monterey Jack or cheddar**
1 cup grits	**Vegetable oil, for frying**

Bring the water or stock and salt to a boil in a 2-quart saucepan. Slowly add the grits, stirring constantly to prevent lumping. Lower the heat to simmer and cover the pot. Let the grits simmer, stirring occasionally, for 20 minutes.

Stir in the cheese and pour the grits into a greased 10-inch pie pan. Let them stand until set. After the grits have stopped steaming, cover them with plastic wrap pressed directly onto their surface. Refrigerate.

When set, cut into wedges, squares, or any shape you want with a cookie cutter. Heat a little vegetable oil in a nonstick skillet over medium-high heat until it is smoking. Carefully add the cutout grits to the pan, without crowding, and fry them until browned and crisp, about 2 minutes. Flip the grits and brown the other side. Don't try to turn the grits over too soon, or they might stick to the pan. Serve hot.

Yield: 6 to 8 servings

The Best Creamed Corn

Creamed corn is one of my favorite things to eat. It seems very comforting to me and is at home on a plate next to the most American of dishes—fried chicken, boiled lobsters, soft-shelled crabs, panfried trout, and similar delights. However, I wouldn't hesitate to serve it with a fancier meal. To round things off, think of something green, like Kale with Bacon and Onion (page 127), or Fried Tomatoes (page 58).

Use fresh corn for the sweetest and most pronounced flavor. Before cutting the kernels off the cob, score the ear lengthwise all the way around with a sharp knife—this will help release the milky juice. For this dish, first cut the top half of the kernels off and then cut them off next to the cob—basically cutting each kernel in half. When all the kernels are off, scrape the cob with the back of your knife to extract every bit of juice.

1 tablespoon unsalted butter	1 large sprig fresh thyme
½ cup diced onion	Small pinch of cayenne pepper
1 teaspoon minced garlic	A few gratings of nutmeg
3 cups fresh corn kernels	Small pinch of curry powder
(about 6 ears)	A grind of black pepper
2 cups heavy cream	Salt to taste
2 bay leaves	Squeeze of fresh lemon juice

Melt the butter in a 2-quart, nonreactive saucepan over medium-low heat. Add the onion and garlic and sweat, stirring occasionally, until softened, about 4 minutes.

Add the corn and continue sweating until the kernels have turned a brighter yellow, about 3 minutes.

Add the cream, bay leaves, thyme, cayenne, nutmeg, curry, and fresh pepper and mix well. Bring to a boil, reduce the heat, and then simmer very gently, stirring often, for 25 minutes. Remove and discard the bay leaves. Season with salt and a squeeze of lemon juice and serve hot.

Yield: 4 servings

Succotash

Succotash is one of those things that has a vaguely bad rep (probably the fault of Sylvester the Cat). In fact, many people don't really know what it is, and even those that do, don't agree. To me, succotash is more of a concept than an exact formula. All it need contain is (good) corn and beans as the Native Americans prepared it, but once you start specifying the type of bean, you're in trouble with somebody. Succotash usually contains lima beans, but sometimes cranberry beans; it can have a bit of tomato or cream, but this draws comments like "Oh no, child!" from some Southerners. All I can say is please yourself—you're the one eating it.

Succotash is a great side dish, in the same category with those comforting southern sides like collard greens and candied yams. It's great with (or under) fish, fried chicken, or pork. Baked sweet potatoes would be an appropriate second side.

1 tablespoon unsalted butter	A grating of nutmeg
¾ cup diced onion	½ cup chicken stock
1 teaspoon minced garlic	1½ cups heavy cream
4 cups cooked beans, such as pinto, pink, or white northerns	2 plum tomatoes, seeded and diced
	Salt and freshly ground pepper to taste
4 cups fresh corn kernels (scrape the cob to get at the juices)	A couple dashes of Tabasco
2 bay leaves	Squeeze of fresh lemon juice

In a heavy 3-quart nonreactive saucepan, heat the butter over medium heat. Add the onion and garlic and cook, stirring occasionally, until softened, about 5 minutes.

Add the beans, corn, bay leaves, nutmeg, stock, and cream. Bring to a boil and then simmer gently for about an hour, stirring occasionally, until all the flavors have mingled and the cream has thickened.

Add the tomatoes, salt, pepper, Tabasco, and lemon juice and simmer another couple of minutes. Discard the bay leaves and serve immediately or let cool a bit and refrigerate.

Yield: 8 servings

Spaetzle

More than one Eastern European country lays claim to originating these delightful little dumplings, made by dropping a thick batter into simmering water or stock. Spaetzle can be served simply boiled, but I love them browned in butter or duck fat. You can also toss them with herbs or fried onions.

Spaetzle are perfect with stews and braised meats; they are just made for sopping up sauce. I wouldn't limit my enjoyment to those dishes, however. Spaetzle is an extremely versatile and benevolent side dish.

2 eggs	A few gratings of nutmeg
½ cup seltzer	A grind of black pepper
1½ cups all-purpose flour	1 tablespoon chopped mixed
½ teaspoon salt	fresh herbs, such as parsley,
¼ teaspoon baking powder	chervil, chives

Beat the eggs and seltzer together in a small bowl.

Sift the flour, salt, baking powder, nutmeg, and pepper together into a mixing bowl and stir in the herbs. Pour the egg mixture into the flour mixture and stir together quickly to form a batter; don't overmix. The batter should be somewhat stiff.

Drop the batter into simmering water or stock by scooping up spoonfuls and scraping off ¼-teaspoon-sized pieces into the simmering liquid. (You can also invest in a specially designed spaetzle maker, a food-mill-type device with large holes, if you take a liking to spaetzle, but it certainly is not necessary.) You will probably have to cook the dumplings in 2 or 3 batches to ensure even cooking times.

The spaetzle are done when they puff a bit and become firmer. Remove the dumplings from the liquid with a slotted spoon and drain. If serving them plain, toss with a little butter so they won't stick together. If sautéing, run the spaetzle under cold water to remove the excess starch and then drain. Sauté them in butter in a very hot pan.

Yield: 4 servings

NOTE: The spaetzle may be made a couple of days in advance. Just cool them with cold water after poaching. Toss with a little oil to prevent them from sticking together and refrigerate.

Sweet Potato Hash with Pecans

Almost any meat or full-flavored fish can share the plate with this hash—beef, chicken, pork, game, turkey, swordfish, trout, and so on—especially if there is some gravy or sauce. Avoid pairing it with very delicately flavored fish, such as sole, or sweet-flavored ones, such as shrimp, because the combination with the sweet potatoes could be cloying. The cream is optional, but it brings out the sweetness of the potatoes more fully.

2 tablespoons unsalted butter

1 onion, peeled and diced

1 garlic clove, minced

2 large sweet potatoes, peeled
   and cut into $\frac{1}{2}$-inch dice

$\frac{1}{2}$ teaspoon kosher salt

A few grinds of black pepper

A few gratings of nutmeg

$\frac{1}{2}$ cup roughly chopped pecans

$\frac{1}{2}$ cup chicken stock or $\frac{1}{4}$ cup
   heavy cream

In a heavy 10-inch skillet, heat the butter over medium heat. Add the onion and garlic and sauté for 1 minute.

Add the sweet potatoes, salt, and pepper, and stir to combine. Pat the mixture down to an even layer, lower the heat a little, and cover. Cook for about 15 minutes, until the potatoes start to become tender.

Uncover the skillet and add the nutmeg, pecans, and chicken stock or cream. Mix well, scraping up any browned bits on the bottom of the skillet. Raise the heat to bring the liquid to a gentle boil and continue boiling until it has completely evaporated, about 5 minutes. Reduce the heat to medium-low and continue cooking the hash, uncovered, until a nice crust has formed on the bottom, about 10 to 15 minutes.

To serve, invert the hash onto a serving platter or just scoop up spoonfuls.

Yield: 2 to 4 servings

Mashed Potatoes with Roasted Garlic and Garlic Chips

No one really needs to be told how to make mashed potatoes or what to serve them with. You know when you need mashed potatoes. This dish is one of those things that everyone has a vehement opinion on. However, the roasted garlic and garlic chips in this preparation give it a different twist. Here the butter and cream have been used in moderation—feel free to add more if you like (I would).

2 heads garlic	½ cup heavy cream or milk
Olive oil, for frying	2 tablespoons unsalted butter
3 Idaho potatoes	Freshly ground pepper to taste
Salt to taste	

Preheat the oven to 300° F.

Remove 6 or 7 of the larger cloves from the heads of garlic and set aside. Rub the remaining whole heads with olive oil, loosely wrap them in foil, and bake for about 1 hour or until the garlic feels soft when you squeeze it. When they are cool enough to handle, cut the heads in half and squeeze out the soft garlic into a mixing bowl. The garlic will have taken on a light golden color.

While the garlic is baking, peel the potatoes, cut them in half, and boil them in salted water until done, about 40 minutes, depending on their size.

While the potatoes are cooking, prepare the garlic chips. Carefully peel each of the reserved garlic cloves, trim off the stem end, and slice thin. Heat about ¼ inch of olive oil in a small frying pan over medium heat. Test the temperature with a slice of garlic—it should sizzle on contact with the oil. Fry the garlic slices in batches, not more than 6 or 8 at a time. Remove from the oil with a slotted spoon as soon as they are golden—if they get too dark they will be bitter. Drain on paper towels and sprinkle with salt. Keep at room temperature. (Save the oil for other uses—it will have a delicious garlic flavor.)

When the potatoes are tender, place them in a bowl with the roasted garlic pulp, cream or milk, and butter. Mash them with a hand masher or electric beater until smooth. Season with salt and pepper. Sprinkle with the garlic chips and serve hot.

Yield: 6 servings

Potato Tots

Pommes dauphinoise *is the proper term for what is recognizable to Americans as the "tater tot." It is a combination of mashed or riced potatoes and Pâte à Choux (cream puff paste). Riced potato makes more "authentic" tots, but I wouldn't hesitate to make them with leftover mashed potatoes. Either way, they are irresistible.*

Serve them at casual meals but also at more formal ones with lamb or steak or at Thanksgiving.

1 pound Idaho potatoes	Salt and freshly ground pepper
¾ cup Pâte à Choux	to taste
(opposite page)	Dry bread crumbs
1 egg yolk	Vegetable oil, for frying
A grating of nutmeg	

Peel the potatoes, place them in a saucepan, and cover them with salted cold water. Bring to a boil and cook them for about 40 minutes or until they are tender when pierced with a fork. Drain.

Mash or rice the cooked potatoes. In a mixing bowl, combine the potato, Pâte à Choux, egg yolk, nutmeg, salt, and pepper and mix very well.

Form the mix into little logs, about ¾ inch by 1½ inches. It is easier to work with your hands a little wet. Dredge each tot in bread crumbs.

Preheat vegetable oil in a fryer or deep heavy skillet to 375°F. Deep-fry the tots in batches, without crowding the pan, until they are golden brown, about 3 minutes. Reserve the cooked tots in a warm oven while you fry the rest. Drain on paper towels and serve.

Yield: 4 servings

NOTE: Potato Tots are perfect for preparing ahead and freezing. After frying, cool the tots and freeze them in a Zip-loc bag. To reheat, place the frozen tots in a 400°F. oven for 10 minutes.

Pâte à Choux

1 cup water or milk

½ cup unsalted butter, cut into bits

⅛ teaspoon salt

1 cup all-purpose flour, sifted

6 eggs, at room temperature

Place the water or milk, butter, and salt in a 2-quart saucepan and bring to a simmer. When the butter has melted, add the flour all at once, stirring constantly. Over low heat, stir the mixture until it forms a ball and the bottom of the pan is coated with a light film.

Place the dough in a mixing bowl and beat the eggs in thoroughly, one by one, with an electric mixer.

NOTE: Pâte à Choux keeps a week in the refrigerator. To store, place the dough in a container and press plastic wrap directly onto the surface of it.

Cumin-Glazed Sweet Potatoes

This rendition of sweet potatoes is irresistible. Serve them with fried or roast chicken, turkey, pork, chicken-fried steak, catfish, or game. A dark leafy green is beautiful with them.

4 sweet potatoes, peeled and cut
    into 1½-inch cubes

1½ teaspoons ground cumin

1 tablespoon unsalted butter, cut
    into bits

¼ cup honey

1 cup chicken stock

Salt and freshly ground pepper
    to taste

Preheat the oven to 350° F.

Combine all the potatoes, cumin, butter, honey, stock, salt, and pepper in a casserole or gratin dish. Stir everything together right in the dish and place it in the oven. Stir the sweet potatoes every once in a while until the liquid has reduced and become dark and syrupy, about 1 hour. Serve immediately.

Yield: 4 servings

Potato Hash with Mushrooms

The mushroom and potato flavors in this hash combine to create a rustic, earthy dish. Serve it with beef, chicken, or game dishes. The Winter Vegetable Purée with Sweet Spices and Crispy Shallots (page 40) would be a delightful accompaniment to the hash.

1 tablespoon unsalted butter	4 Idaho potatoes, peeled and cut
½ cup diced onion	into ½-inch dice
2 cups quartered mushrooms	Salt and freshly ground pepper to
2 teaspoons minced garlic	taste
	1 teaspoon chopped fresh thyme

In a heavy 10-inch skillet, preferably cast-iron, heat the butter over medium heat. Add the onion and mushrooms and sauté, stirring occasionally, until they are lightly browned—about 10 minutes. Stir in the garlic and sauté for another minute.

Add the potatoes to the skillet, season with salt and pepper, and mix well. You may have to add more butter at this point. Turn the heat down to low, cover the pan, and cook the hash for about 15 minutes, until a crust has started to form and the potatoes are just cooked through.

Remove the cover, add the fresh thyme, and stir the hash, scraping up the browned bits from the bottom and mixing them into the hash. Press down gently on the hash to even it out. Raise the heat a little and continue cooking the hash until it is browned on the bottom, another 10 minutes. Serve directly from the pan or turn it out onto a platter.

Yield: 4 servings

My Grandmother's Orzo

My grandmother used to prepare this dish with browned chicken cooked right into it, and she called it Greek chicken. She made it quite often, as I remember, and I loved it, although I was a finicky eater.

Without the chicken it becomes an excellent side dish. It is best if eaten soon after cooking, but it can be refrigerated and reheated gently, with some water, in a skillet.

2 tablespoons olive oil	½ teaspoon dried oregano
1 tablespoon minced garlic	½ teaspoon dried thyme
1 small onion, diced	5 grinds of black pepper
1½ cups uncooked orzo	Salt to taste
4 canned tomatoes, very roughly chopped	Tiny pinch of ground cloves
	½ cinnamon stick
2½ cups chicken stock	Tiny pinch of cayenne pepper

In a 2-quart sauce pan, heat the olive oil over medium heat. Add the garlic and onion and sauté lightly, stirring often, until they are soft, but not browned—about 5 minutes.

Add the orzo to the pot and sauté it for 1 minute, stirring. Add the tomatoes, stock, oregano, thyme, pepper, salt, cloves, cinnamon, and cayenne and stir to combine.

Bring the liquid to a boil and then reduce the heat to low and cook the orzo until tender, about 10 minutes. Be sure to stir often or the pasta will stick to the bottom of the pot. Remove the cinnamon stick and serve hot.

Yield: 4 servings

Salad
Sides

Although salads are often served on their own, either as a separate course or as a light entrée, they have their place on the dinner plate as well. Their refreshing, bright flavors, sometimes with a bit of a crunch, can offer a pleasing contrast to the main course. Salads also give the cook a creative opportunity to blend ingredients, textures, and flavors that perfectly complement the entrée and other side dishes. If a meal has many round flavors in it, such as cream, cheese, or meat, the sharpness of a vinaigrette or the green crunch of a raw julienned snow pea can liven things up. If there are meat juices or barbecue sauce on the plate, the creamy dressing of a potato salad or cole slaw can be just the thing to mingle with it.

Another admirable quality of salads is their simplicity. If you are planning a meal with several dishes and just want an uncomplicated vegetable to go alongside, steamed or blanched vegetables with a light dressing can complete the picture. And, of course, there is nothing like a buffet or an outdoor meal consisting of a simple main course and many side salads. In fact, if the salads are varied and zesty enough, you can just forget the entrée altogether.

Japanese Mushroom Salad ◆ *Julienned Snow Peas with Sesame Oil* ◆ *Tomato and Avocado Salsa* ◆ *Spicy Seaweed Salad* ◆ *Red Cabbage Slaw* ◆ *Backyard Coleslaw* ◆ *Green and Yellow Bean Salad with Shallot Vinaigrette* ◆ *Chilled Spinach Salad with Hot Pepper, Garlic, and Soy Sauce* ◆ *Bulgur Salad with Orange, Radish, and Mint* ◆ *Warm Curried Lentil Salad* ◆ *Chilled Lentils with Extra Virgin Olive Oil and Parsley* ◆ *Black Bean Salad with Red Onion and Cilantro Vinaigrette* ◆ *Couscous Salad with Cilantro and Lime Juice* ◆ *Orvietta Salad with Olives, Sun-Dried Tomatoes, and Capers* ◆ *Fusilli Salad with Snow Peas and Red Peppers* ◆ *Potato Salad, Picnic Style* ◆ *New Potato Salad with Creamy Whole-Grain Mustard Dressing* ◆ *Warm New Potato Salad with Dill* ◆ *Baby New Potato Salad with Bacon and Chives*

Japanese Mushroom Salad

The light and slightly sweet dressing in this recipe allows one to fully appreciate the delicate earthiness of cultivated button mushrooms. This salad should be consumed within a couple of hours of making it, before the dressing saturates the mushrooms. Try it in the spring or summer with simple grilled foods or sandwiches.

The ingredients for the dressing can be found in shops that specialize in Asian products.

3 tablespoons mirin (Japanese sweet rice cooking wine)

¼ cup rice vinegar

1 tablespoon soy sauce

3 tablespoons *dashi* (Japanese fish stock) or water

12 large cultivated button mushrooms, thinly sliced

Combine the mirin, rice vinegar, soy sauce, and *dashi* or water. Gently toss the mushrooms in the dressing and serve immediately.

Yield: 2 to 4 servings

Julienned Snow Peas with Sesame Oil

This dish can be prepared in minutes. Snow peas are as delicious raw as they are cooked. Serve this dish with cold meat salads or sandwiches or next to sautéed shrimp.

½ pound snow peas

2 tablespoons Asian sesame oil

1 teaspoon rice vinegar

½ teaspoon soy sauce

⅛ teaspoon hot red pepper flakes

Salt to taste

String the snow peas and then cut them lengthwise into thin strips.

In a mixing bowl, combine the sesame oil, rice vinegar, soy sauce, red pepper flakes, and the salt. Add the julienned snow peas and toss. Serve immediately or refrigerate.

Yield: 2 to 4 servings

Tomato and Avocado Salsa

This salsa is chunky enough when first made to serve as a side dish for grilled or sautéed foods. If not consumed right after preparation it becomes more of a dip or sauce, which is also great but hard to get your fork into. It is imperative that you make this with ripe tomatoes—it's pointless otherwise.

I might serve Curried Potato Chips (page 71) or Mashed Potatoes with Roasted Garlic and Garlic Chips (page 141) or any of the black bean dishes (pages 66, 134, and 158) with it.

4 cups fresh plum tomatoes, seeded and cut into ½-inch dice	1 small jalapeño, diced very small
	Juice of 2 limes
1 small onion, peeled and cut into small dice	Salt and freshly ground pepper to taste
½ cup chopped fresh coriander	1 ripe Haas avocado

Combine the tomatoes, onion, coriander, jalapeño, lime juice, salt, and pepper in a nonreactive bowl and mix well. When ready to serve, cut and add the avocado. The acids from the tomato and lime juice preserve the color of the avocado pretty well, but it's better to add it at the last moment all the same.

Yield: 8 servings

Spicy Seaweed Salad

Seaweed is often overlooked by Occidentals, but it is delicious, healthful, and widely available in health-food and Asian markets. In fact, once you look for it you will probably be surprised at the diversity of packaged seaweeds you will find. For this salad, I chose hijiki, *a dark, twiglike variety with a mild flavor. Its blackness creates a stunning presentation when paired with bright green vegetables like snow peas or sugar snaps.*

Seaweed is a natural with fish dishes, but also has a surprising affinity for mushrooms. Try it with a fish or light meat dish with a mushroom sauce or side dish.

1½ ounces dried *hijiki* seaweed	3 tablespoons rice vinegar
2 tablespoon light soy sauce,	1 teaspoon Asian sesame oil
preferably Japanese (see Note)	2 scallions, minced
1 tablespoon mirin (see Note)	½ teaspoon hot red pepper flakes

Soak the *hijiki* in a bowl of cold water until softened, about 15 minutes. Drain, rinse, and drain again.

Combine the soy sauce, mirin, rice vinegar, sesame oil, scallions, and pepper flakes in a bowl and mix well. Add the *hijiki* and toss. This can be served right away but is better if left for an hour or so in the refrigerator.

Yield: 4 servings

NOTE: Soy sauce comes in varying flavors and strengths. Light soy sauce is a light-bodied style, not a low-sodium one. Substitute regular soy sauce if you cannot find light soy.

Mirin is a sweet rice wine that is used in many Japanese dishes and is available in Asian and health-food markets.

Red Cabbage Slaw

Coleslaw is great picnic food, but also makes frequent indoor appearances alongside sandwiches, fried chicken, pork chops, and the like. I think this particular slaw would be good with duck, too. Serve a potato dish without cream with it and some sautéed string beans, snow peas, or sugar snaps.

1 tablespoon Dijon mustard	1 medium onion, peeled and diced
½ cup mayonnaise	½ cup diced green apple
1 teaspoon minced garlic	1 carrot, shredded
2 teaspoons white wine vinegar	Salt and freshly ground pepper
4 cups shredded red cabbage	to taste

Place the mustard, mayonnaise, garlic, and vinegar in a bowl large enough to hold all the slaw. Stir well to combine.

Add the cabbage, onion, apple, and carrot and mix well. Season liberally with the salt and pepper and toss thoroughly. Serve chilled.

Yield: 4 to 6 servings

NOTE: This keeps 2 or 3 days in the refrigerator and is better if made a couple of hours ahead.

Backyard Coleslaw

This is your basic coleslaw, happy at a picnic or barbecue. It's also wonderful right on a meatloaf or turkey sandwich. I like to let coleslaw sit awhile before serving—it gives the cabbage a chance to relax.

2 cups mayonnaise	1 carrot, grated
4 teaspoons sugar	1 onion, cut into small dice
1½ teaspoons Colman's mustard	Salt and freshly ground pepper
4 tablespoons white wine vinegar	to taste
8 cups shredded cabbage	

In a large mixing bowl, whisk together the mayonnaise, sugar, mustard, and vinegar.

Add the cabbage, carrot, onion, salt, and pepper and mix well. Refrigerate for an hour or so before serving.

Yield: 8 to 10 servings

Green and Yellow Bean Salad with Shallot Vinaigrette

This is a good all-purpose salad that fits in nicely with more complicated side dishes. It can be tailored by adding herbs such as chives, chervil, basil, mint, or thyme and by using fresh lemon juice or white or red wine vinegar for the dressing. Sometimes I also crumble a little feta or mild goat cheese over the top.

¼ cup finely diced shallot	Salt and freshly ground pepper
¼ cup white wine vinegar	to taste
½ cup olive oil	1 pound mixed green and yellow
	beans

Whisk together the shallot, vinegar, olive oil, salt, and pepper. It is best to do this an hour or so ahead to let the shallot flavor seep into the dressing.

Blanch the beans in salted, boiling water until just done—keep them crisp. Drain and refresh under cold water.

Arrange the beans on a serving platter. Just before serving, pour the dressing over the beans and toss. Serve at room temperature.

Yield: 4 servings

NOTE: The dressing should always be added at the last moment for the best appearance. The acid in the dressing turns the green beans olive green after a while, although the flavor is still fine.

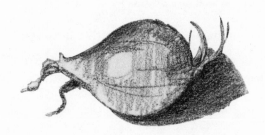

Chilled Spinach Salad with Hot Pepper, Garlic, and Soy Sauce

This is a refreshing, slightly spicy salad suitable for serving with stir-fries, simple roasts, or sautéed meats, sandwiches, and some noodle dishes in which the flavors won't clash. It's great as part of a buffet. Serve this salad within 24 hours, because its color becomes less attractive over time.

2 large bunches curly spinach (about 2 pounds), steamed and chilled (page 130)

¼ cup vegetable oil

3 garlic cloves, peeled and thinly sliced

½ cup soy sauce

2 teaspoons Asian sesame oil

¼ teaspoon hot red pepper flakes

While the spinach is chilling, prepare the dressing. Heat the vegetable oil in a small skillet over medium heat. It is hot enough when a slice of garlic dropped in the oil immediately sizzles. Fry the garlic slices in 2 or 3 batches until lightly browned. (Reserve the garlic oil for another use.) Place the fried garlic in a bowl big enough to hold all the spinach.

Add the soy sauce, sesame oil, and hot red pepper flakes to the bowl and whisk together. Add a bit of cold water to dilute the dressing to your taste. When the spinach is chilled, toss with the dressing.

Yield: 4 servings

Bulgur Salad with Orange, Radish, and Mint

Bulgur, or cracked wheat, is the main ingredient in the now-familiar tabbouleh salad. It is quite simple to prepare, requiring only a preliminary soaking to tenderize the grain. To save time you can cook the bulgur over low heat—how long it will take depends on how coarse your bulgur is, but figure about 20 minutes. Let the bulgar stand for a little while off the heat after the water is absorbed, to let it dry out. Cool it quickly by spreading it out on a cookie sheet and refrigerating.

This salad is healthful and refreshing, the nutty, earthy taste of the bulgur sweetened a bit by the orange, with radish and cucumber adding crunch. Serve it as part of a buffet, with sandwiches, or next to chicken, pork, or game. It's not likely to clash with much. For a second side dish, the Rosemary-Scented Roasted Carrots, Turnips, and Shallots (page 23) or Provençal Broiled Tomatoes (page 10) would be especially pleasing.

2 cups bulgur	**2 tablespoons chopped Italian**
6 cups cold water	**parsley**
3 navel oranges	**Juice of 2 lemons**
8 radishes	**¼ cup extra virgin olive oil**
1 cucumber	**Salt and freshly ground pepper**
3 tablespoons chopped fresh mint	**to taste**

Place the bulgur in a large bowl. Cover with the cold water and let sit for 90 minutes or until the bulgur is tender to your taste. Pour off any unabsorbed water and let the bulgur drain in a colander. When it seems dry, return it to the bowl.

Cut the orange into segments by cutting off the peel and pith with a sharp knife. Cut in between the membranes to free the sections. Add the orange sections to the bulgur and squeeze the juice from the orange membranes over the bulgur as well.

Cut the radishes in half and then slice into half-moons. Add them to the bulgur.

Cut the cucumber into large dice and add it to the bulgur. Add the mint and parsley and mix everything together. Season with the lemon juice, olive oil, salt, and pepper. Serve immediately or refrigerate and serve chilled.

Yield: 6 to 8 servings

Warm Curried Lentil Salad

These lentils are pleasing in their mild curry flavor and pretty colors. Serve them with grilled sausages, lamb chops, duck confit, sandwiches, or as part of a buffet.

1 cup dried lentils	**¼ cup white wine vinegar**
½ cup olive oil	**1½ teaspoons salt**
¼ cup small-diced onion	**4 grinds of black pepper**
¼ cup small-diced carrots	**¼ cup coarsely chopped Italian**
1 tablespoon curry powder	**parsley**
Juice of 1 lemon	

In a saucepan, cover the lentils with cold water and bring to a boil over high heat. Lower the heat to maintain a steady simmer and cook the lentils until tender, about 40 minutes. Drain.

In a 10-inch sauté pan, heat the olive oil over low heat and add the onion and carrots. Cook gently for about 3 minutes, until the vegetables are softened somewhat.

Stir in the curry powder and cook for another minute. Be careful not to scorch the curry powder.

Add the lemon juice, white wine vinegar, salt, and pepper. Stir well to combine.

Add the lentils and stir until they are warmed through, about 4 minutes. Stir in the parsley and adjust the seasonings.

Yield: 6 servings

NOTE: Leftover curried lentils can be eaten cold or reheated slowly over a gentle flame.

Chilled Lentils with Extra Virgin Olive Oil and Parsley

This salad is appropriate to any season, served alongside a sandwich, simple meat dish, or as part of a group of salads. It may be kept in the refrigerator, but be sure to let the salad stand at room temperature a little while before serving to let the olive oil relax.

⅔ cup dried lentils

¼ cup white wine vinegar

½ cup extra virgin olive oil

1 teaspoon salt

3 grinds of black pepper

½ cup coarsely chopped Italian parsley

In a saucepan, cover the lentils with cold water and bring to a boil over high heat. Reduce the heat and simmer the lentils until tender, about 40 minutes. Drain and cool.

In a bowl, combine the white wine vinegar, olive oil, salt, pepper, and parsley. Whisk well to combine.

Stir in the cooked lentils. Taste and adjust the seasonings. Serve slightly chilled.

Yield: 4 servings

Black Bean Salad with Red Onion and Cilantro Vinaigrette

This salad is quick to make and can be served with a wide range of entrées, from grilled steak to marinated chicken breasts. Try it as part of a summertime buffet or light lunch, pairing it with a tomato or corn salad, perhaps.

¼ cup plus 1 tablespoon sherry vinegar

¼ cup olive oil

⅓ cup chopped fresh cilantro

3 cups cooked black beans

½ cup diced red onion

Salt and freshly ground pepper to taste

Place the vinegar in a bowl. Add the olive oil in a slow stream, whisking continually. Stir in the cilantro.

Add the black beans and red onion and stir to combine. Season with the salt and pepper.

Yield: 4 to 6 servings

NOTE: This salad keeps well in the refrigerator and, in fact, is better when made a day ahead. Bring to room temperature before serving.

Couscous Salad with Cilantro and Lime Juice

This colorful salad would be perfect as part of a buffet. I like it with grilled foods of any kind—steak, pork chops, chicken, fish, shrimp, or vegetables. It also pairs well with Mexican or Middle Eastern flavors. As an accompanying side dish I would choose a green vegetable, anything from Broccoli Tempura (page 61) to sautéed string beans. If picking a third side dish, try a black bean or chickpea dish.

1½ cups uncooked couscous	3 tablespoons finely diced carrots
6 tablespoons olive oil	3 tablespoons finely diced zucchini
½ cup very hot water	1 small shallot, finely diced
3 tablespoons fresh lime juice	Salt and freshly ground pepper
3 tablespoons coarsely chopped	to taste
fresh cilantro	

Toss the couscous with 1 tablespoon of olive oil, thoroughly coating each grain. Pour the very hot water over the couscous and stir until the water is absorbed. Let sit for 2 minutes.

With a fork, stir another tablespoon of olive oil into the couscous. Set aside to cool.

Whisk together the lime juice and remaining 4 tablespoons of olive oil. Combine the couscous, dressing, cilantro, carrots, zucchini, shallot, and salt and pepper, mixing well. Serve immediately or refrigerate.

Yield: 4 servings

NOTE: This will keep at least several days in the refrigerator—just be sure to serve it at room temperature.

Orvietta Salad with Olives, Sun-Dried Tomatoes, and Capers

Pasta salads make a good all-around dish. You can vary the ingredients according to your whim, tailoring them to suit the entrée you are serving. This one contains a number of piquant items, which I believe to be appetite stimulating. Sometimes I add smoked mozzarella if the pasta salad is to be part of a larger meal with more dishes. Serve this with simple sautés or roasts and choose either of the radicchio side dishes (pages 51 and 82), Provençal Broiled Tomatoes (page 10), or Snow Pea Parallelograms with Shiitakes (page 14) to complement it. This may be made a day ahead; just be sure to bring it to room temperature before serving.

1 pound uncooked orvietta pasta	¼ cup extra virgin olive oil
1 cup black olives, preferably Kalamata or Moroccan	¼ cup pure olive oil
	1 tablespoon minced garlic
½ cup oil-packed sun-dried tomatoes	½ cup shredded fresh basil
	¼ cup small capers
½ pound smoked mozzarella (optional)	Salt and freshly ground pepper to taste
¼ cup white wine vinegar	

Cook the pasta in boiling salted water for about 15 minutes or until al dente. (If the salad is not to be served immediately, make the pasta a little more al dente than you might ordinarily, because it will absorb the dressing and become softer as it sits.) Drain and cool under cold running water, then drain again.

While the pasta is cooking, pit the olives by pressing down on them with the palm of your hand, which will split them open, and then removing the exposed pits. Cut the olives in half.

Cut the sun-dried tomatoes into 3 or 4 pieces each.

If using mozzarella, cut it into ½-inch dice.

Whisk together the vinegar, olive oils, garlic, and basil in a small bowl. In a mixing bowl, combine the cooked pasta, olives, capers, sun-dried tomatoes, dressing, and salt and pepper and mix thoroughly. Taste, and adjust the seasonings. Serve immediately or refrigerate.

Yield: 6 to 8 servings

Fusilli Salad with Snow Peas and Red Peppers

Fusilli, or corkscrew, pasta has a fun shape that holds julienned vegetables well. It is best to prepare this salad close to serving time in order to retain the fresh green color of the snow peas and parsley.

For suggestions on serving pasta salads, please see the introduction to Orvietta Salad with Olives, Sun-Dried Tomatoes, and Capers (opposite).

1 pound uncooked fusilli	2 teaspoons minced garlic
4 ounces snow peas	Salt and freshly ground pepper
1 large red bell pepper	to taste
¼ cup white wine vinegar	1 bunch Italian parsley,
½ cup olive oil	coarsely chopped

Cook the pasta in boiling salted water for about 15 minutes or until al dente. Drain and cool under cold running water, then drain again.

While the pasta is boiling, prepare the vegetables. String the snow peas and cut them lengthwise into thin strips. Remove the stem, seeds, and pith from the red pepper and cut it into thin strips the same size as the snow peas.

In a small bowl, whisk together the white wine vinegar, olive oil, garlic, salt, pepper, and parsley.

Place the cooked, cooled pasta in a large bowl and pour the dressing over it. Add the julienned vegetables and mix everything together. Taste, and adjust the seasonings. Serve at room temperature.

Yield: 6 to 8 servings

Potato Salad, Picnic Style

This is my favorite potato salad. It's great with sandwiches and barbecue or just to have on hand for a snack. Sometimes I add some chopped hard-boiled egg or chopped sweet pickles, depending on my mood. Cooking the potatoes in their jackets gives them a fuller, more earthy flavor.

6 Idaho potatoes, scrubbed	½ teaspoon freshly ground black
3 tablespoons kosher salt	pepper
1 onion, cut into small dice	Pinch of cayenne pepper
(about ¾ cup)	1½ cups mayonnaise
1 tablespoon dry mustard,	Dash of white wine vinegar
preferably Colman's	Mild paprika, for dusting

Put the potatoes in a large pot with cold water to cover and 2 tablespoons of the kosher salt. Bring to a boil, then lower the heat to sustain a moderate boil and cook the potatoes until a knife pierces them easily, about 1 hour. Drain.

When the potatoes are cool enough to handle, peel them and cut them into ½-inch cubes.

In a bowl, combine the diced potatoes with the onion, mustard, pepper, cayenne, mayonnaise, vinegar, and the remaining tablespoon of salt (or salt to taste). Mix well. Serve chilled, dusted lightly with paprika.

Yield: 6 to 8 servings

New Potato Salad with Creamy Whole-Grain Mustard Dressing

Another version of potato salad, this time with the bite of mustard and a whisper of tarragon. Serve it as part of a barbecue, or with steak, chicken, or pork. Since the dressing is somewhat creamy, I would avoid partnering this with dishes with cream in them—save this salad for something more simple, with just good meat juices to run into the salad. Accompany it with sautéed kale, Rosemary-Scented Roasted Carrots, Turnips, and Shallots (page 23), or Green and Yellow Bean Salad with Shallot Vinaigrette (page 154).

12 red or white new potatoes	½ teaspoon minced garlic
½ cup sour cream	1 teaspoon chopped fresh tarragon
½ cup mayonnaise	1 tablespoon milk or heavy cream
3 tablespoons whole-grain mustard	Salt to taste

In a saucepan, cover the potatoes with salted cold water and bring to a boil. Cook them at a low boil for about 30 minutes, until tender when pierced with a fork. Drain and cool.

While the potatoes are cooking, prepare the dressing. In a medium bowl, combine the sour cream, mayonnaise, mustard, garlic, tarragon, milk or cream, and salt, and mix well.

Cut the potatoes into halves or quarters, depending on their size. Toss them with the dressing and serve immediately or refrigerate. Serve chilled.

Yield: 4 to 6 servings

NOTE: This may be made a day ahead.

Warm New Potato Salad with Dill

Try this salad with pork roast or chops or sautéed chicken breasts. It also goes well with Braised Leeks (page 20) or Apple Fritters (page 60).

8 red new potatoes	**⅓ cup coarsely chopped fresh dill**
1 tablespoon white wine vinegar	**Salt and freshly ground pepper to**
2 tablespoons olive oil	**taste**

Wash the potatoes and boil them in salted water for 30 to 35 minutes, until tender when pierced with a fork.

Drain the potatoes, and as soon as you can handle them, cut them into ½-inch slices. Place the slices in a serving bowl.

Immediately sprinkle with the vinegar and toss gently. Drizzle with the olive oil, dill, salt, and pepper, and toss again. Serve immediately.

Yield: 2 to 4 servings

Baby New Potato Salad with Bacon and Chives

Every year I look forward to the arrival of spring and, with it, the year's first baby new potatoes. Their nice waxy texture and tender skin make them ideal for potato salads to serve at those early barbecues. As with Potato Salad, Picnic Style (page 162), I like to serve this salad with something barbecued; I particularly like the melding of barbecue sauce and mayonnaise on the plate. Sandwiches or simple dishes also make a good main dish. Green beans or a little green salad is all that is needed to round off a meal like this.

8 new potatoes, preferably red	2 tablespoons fresh chives, cut in
6 strips bacon, cut into ½-inch	1-inch lengths
pieces	Salt and freshly ground pepper to
Scant ½ cup mayonnaise	taste

In a saucepan, cover the potatoes with salted cold water and bring to a boil. Cook them at a low boil for about 30 minutes, until tender when pierced with a fork. Drain and cool.

While the potatoes are cooking, place the bacon strips in a small skillet and cook over medium-low heat until they are quite crisp, about 10 minutes. Drain off the fat and reserve it for another use. Crumble the bacon into a mixing bowl.

When the potatoes are cool, cut them into 4 or 6 pieces depending on how you like your salad. Place them in the bowl with the bacon, add the mayonnaise, chives, salt, and pepper, and toss. Serve immediately or chill.

Yield: 2 to 4 servings

NOTE: This keeps for several days in the refrigerator.

Breads, Crackers, and Other Baked Sides

reads are not often thought of as a side dish, yet they can take many different forms, most of which are a terrific addition to a meal. Nestle a few just-baked crackers or Parmesan sticks alongside a steaming bowl of soup to make it a full and satisfying meal. Split open a hot biscuit or popover to sop up delicious stew juices. Serve crepes or johnnycakes, types of pancakes that are excellent with dinner.

Including small touches like these in a meal will produce delight in your family and guests and make them think you have gone to a lot of trouble for them. In reality, these recipes are relatively simple and quick to do as well as inexpensive. And they make your house smell good, too!

Johnnycakes ◆ *Parmesan Spoonbread* ◆ *Wild Turkey Stuffing Cake* ◆ *Wild Rice Waffles* ◆ *Crepes* ◆ *Bacon Cornsticks* ◆ *Basic Biscuits* ◆ *Cheddar Biscuits* ◆ *Ham and Black Pepper Biscuits* ◆ *Popovers* ◆ *Feather Dumplings* ◆ *Texas Toast* ◆ *Parmesan Twists* ◆ *Corn-Chili Crackers* ◆ *Poppy-Oat Crackers* ◆ *Sesame Crackers* ◆ *Cheese Straws* ◆ *Goat Cheese Toasts*

Johnnycakes

True Rhode Island johnnycakes are made with white cornmeal, but I wouldn't let that stop me if all I had on hand was the yellow variety. These are nice little corn pancakes to serve next to a creamed chicken dish or a seafood dinner. I love them with sautéed soft-shelled crabs. They're also nice drizzled with a little maple syrup.

1 cup all-purpose flour	3 eggs
1 cup cornmeal	¼ cup (½ stick) unsalted butter,
2 teaspoons baking powder	melted and at room
¼ teaspoon salt	temperature
2 cups milk	

Sift the flour, cornmeal, baking powder, and salt into a mixing bowl.

Beat together the milk, eggs, and melted butter.

Pour the liquid ingredients into the dry and stir until just combined. Don't overmix. The batter should be a bit thinner than regular pancake batter.

Spoon the batter onto a greased griddle or frying pan, forming thin pancakes 2½ inches in diameter. Cook the johnnycakes over moderate heat until bubbles form and burst on the surface, and the bottom is golden brown, 1 to 2 minutes. Turn the johnnycakes and cook the other side for 1 minute, until speckled.

Yield: 6 to 8 servings

NOTE: Johnnycakes can be kept in a warm oven while the rest are being cooked.

Parmesan Spoonbread

Spoonbread is a classic American dish that originated in the South. They are like a souffléed polenta. Spoonbreads can be flavored with herbs, cheese, cracklings, or chili powder and made with butter, chicken fat, or duck fat—giving the cook an opportunity to tailor the seasonings to the main course.

2 cups milk or chicken stock	2 tablespoons unsalted butter
Salt and freshly ground pepper to taste	3 eggs, separated
1 cup cornmeal	⅓ cup plus 1 tablespoon grated Parmesan

Preheat a 1-quart baking dish, cast-iron skillet, or casserole in a 375°F. oven.

In a heavy-bottomed 2-quart saucepan, combine the milk or stock, salt, and pepper. Bring the mixture to a boil over high heat. Lower the heat and while the milk is simmering sift in the cornmeal, holding the sifter or strainer in one hand and stirring rapidly with the other. When the cornmeal is incorporated, continue stirring for another 2 minutes over low heat until a thick but creamy consistency is achieved. If the mixture becomes too thick and starts to form a single mass, add a little more liquid.

Remove the batter from the heat and stir in the butter. Slowly add the egg yolks and finally stir in ⅓ cup of the Parmesan. Taste and adjust the seasonings.

In a mixing bowl, beat the egg whites until stiff peaks form. Add a large spoonful of the egg whites to the cornmeal mixture and mix well to lighten it. Then in 3 batches, fold the cornmeal mixture into the remaining egg whites.

Take the preheated baking dish out of the oven and liberally coat the interior with butter. Pour in the spoonbread batter and sprinkle the top with the remaining tablespoon of Parmesan. Bake until the spoonbread has risen and is nicely browned, about 40 minutes. Serve immediately.

Yield: 4 to 6 servings

Wild Turkey Stuffing Cake

This is a fun side dish to make when you aren't cooking a bird but are in the mood for stuffing. Pair it with Creamed Spinach (page 129) or Sautéed Mushrooms with Oregano (page 8).

1 large loaf Italian bread	1 egg
3 tablespoons unsalted butter	$\frac{1}{2}$ cup chicken stock
1 cup diced onion	1 tablespoon Wild Turkey or other
1 teaspoon minced garlic	bourbon
1 teaspoon dried thyme	Salt and freshly ground pepper
$\frac{1}{2}$ teaspoon dried sage	to taste

Preheat the oven to 350° F.

Trim the crust from the bread and cut it into $\frac{1}{2}$-inch cubes.

Melt 1 tablespoon of the butter in a 10-inch sauté pan over medium heat. Add half the bread cubes and toss. Let them toast, tossing occasionally, until they are golden. Remove the croutons to a bowl. Add another tablespoon of butter to the pan and repeat with the rest of the bread.

Melt the last tablespoon of butter in the pan. Add the onion and cook, stirring occasionally, until it is softened and very lightly browned, about 5 minutes.

Add the garlic, thyme, and sage and cook, stirring, for another minute. Remove everything to the bowl with the croutons.

Add the egg, stock, bourbon, salt, and pepper to the bowl and mix well. Pack into a greased 4-cup loaf pan. Cover with foil and bake for 15 minutes. Remove the foil and bake another 20 to 25 minutes, until the top has formed a nice crust. Unmold and slice.

Yield: 2 to 4 servings

Wild Rice Waffles

Waffles are an old-fashioned American side dish. Creamed chicken on waffles typifies a certain nook of American cuisine, one that is making a comeback. Wild rice adds a nutty flavor to the waffles and dresses them up a bit. It can be left out entirely, however, or nuts or herbs substituted. These waffles would be delicious with game birds, especially if there's a creamy sauce to sop. If there isn't, try serving them with a creamy side dish, like Creamed Spinach (page 129).

1 cup all-purpose flour	¾ cup milk
1 teaspoon baking powder	2½ tablespoons butter, melted and
¼ teaspoon salt	at room temperature
2 tablespoons roughly chopped	1 egg
cooked wild rice	

Preheat the waffle iron.

Sift the dry ingredients into a mixing bowl. Stir in the wild rice.

Combine the liquids and egg in another bowl and whisk well. Pour the liquids into the dry ingredients all at once and mix just enough to combine—don't overmix.

Bake in the waffle iron until golden brown. Serve immediately.

Yield: 4 waffles

NOTE: These can be cooled and frozen; reheat in a 350°F. oven for 5 to 7 minutes.

Crepes

For more tender crepes, prepare the batter at least an hour ahead, or preferably overnight, to allow the gluten in the flour to relax. Crepe batter will keep for 2 days, refrigerated.

2 small eggs	¼ cup all-purpose flour
½ cup water	1 tablespoon mixed chopped fresh
1½ teaspoons olive oil	herbs, such as chives, chervil,
Dash of brandy	parsley, thyme (optional)
Salt and freshly ground pepper	Oil or clarified butter (page 79),
to taste	for brushing

In a mixing bowl, combine the eggs, water, oil, brandy, salt, and pepper and whisk well.

Add the flour and whisk just enough to work out most of the lumps. If time permits, let the batter rest for at least an hour. Add the herbs if using and stir to combine.

Heat an 8-inch omelette or crepe pan until it starts to smoke. Brush it very lightly with oil or clarified butter. Remove the pan from the heat and pour in about 2 tablespoons of batter, tilting the pan as you do so that the batter lightly coats the bottom of the pan. Place the pan back on the burner and cook the crepe for 20 to 30 seconds, until lightly speckled on the bottom. Turn it over and cook the other side about 10 seconds and then slide the crepe out of the pan onto a plate. Be careful not to overcook the crepe, or it will become brittle. Repeat until all the batter is used up.

Yield: 8 to 10 crepes

NOTE: The cooked crepes can be stacked, well wrapped, and frozen. They thaw quickly.

VARIATION

Wild Rice Crepes may be made by adding ¼ cup of coarsely chopped cooked wild rice to the batter.

Bacon Cornsticks

These are quite fun and are at home at a picnic or barbecue, with fried chicken or southern stews. They look great fanned upright in a napkin-lined basket.

If you lack a cornstick mold, just use a 10-inch cast-iron frying pan or other baking dish and cut the corn bread in wedges to serve.

5 strips bacon, cut crosswise at
   ¼-inch intervals
1 cup all-purpose flour
1 cup cornmeal
1 tablespoon baking powder
½ teaspoon salt
½ cup finely chopped onion

¾ cup milk
¼ cup heavy cream
¼ cup (½ stick) unsalted butter,
   melted, at room temperature
1 tablespoon honey
2 eggs

Preheat the oven to 425°F.

Fry the bacon in a 10-inch skillet over medium heat until it is crisp—about 10 minutes. Drain the bacon on paper towels and reserve the fat. While the bacon is frying, heat your cornstick mold in the preheated 425°F. oven.

Sift the dry ingredients together into a bowl and stir in the onion.

Combine the liquids and eggs in another mixing bowl and whisk well.

Pour the wet ingredients into the dry mixture and stir just until moistened; don't over-mix the batter.

Remove the mold from the oven and brush each depression with bacon fat. Sprinkle in some of the bacon bits and then spoon in the batter, filling to just below the rim. Bake until the cornsticks are golden brown on the bottom, about 15 minutes. Remove the cornsticks immediately from the mold and keep warm; repeat the process, using the rest of the bacon bits and batter.

Yield: 12 cornsticks

NOTE: The cornsticks are best right from the oven and really should be eaten the same day they are made.

Basic Biscuits

Biscuits are a delightful, unpretentious side dish, ready to nestle up to your fried chicken or gumbo and wallow in the gravy. They are quick and easy to make.

While biscuits prepared in this southern style have a natural place next to homey comfort foods like fried chicken, pork chops, or BBQ, a few small touches can deem them appropriate for more elegant meals. Try making miniature biscuits, sprinkled with cracked pepper or herbs, to serve on the plate alongside rack of lamb, for instance. Let your imagination guide you.

2 cups all-purpose flour

4 teaspoons baking powder

1 teaspoon salt

½ cup (1 stick) very cold unsalted
    butter, cut into ½-inch pieces

¾ cup milk

Melted butter, for brushing
    (optional)

Flour, for dusting (optional)

Preheat the oven to 400° F.

Combine the flour, baking powder, and salt in a mixing bowl. Add the butter and work it quickly with your fingertips, breaking it into smaller pieces. Leave a few pieces larger than you think you should—these will make the biscuits nice and buttery.

Add the milk to the bowl and stir it in with a spoon. The dough should be wet but not too sticky; it should be rollable. If it is too dry, add a little more milk.

Flour a work surface and turn the dough out onto it. Sprinkle the dough with a little flour and roll it out to about ¾ inch thick. Dust off the top and fold it in thirds. Roll it out again ¾ inch thick. Cut the dough into any size biscuits you want—if making miniatures, I'd roll out the dough to ½ inch thick.

Place the biscuits on a greased baking sheet. You can make more choices here. You may brush them with melted butter if you wish or dust them with flour or do nothing at all. You can either space them so they are not touching, or crowd them together so the sides come out soft. At any rate, bake them for about 15 minutes, until they have risen and are lightly browned. The sooner you eat them the better.

Yield: 10 to 12 3-inch biscuits

NOTE: Serve the biscuits on the side in a basket if you wish, but I like to split them and serve them right on the plate with some gravy, be it brown or white.

Cheddar Biscuits

Use the sharpest cheddar you can find—the flavor of mild cheddar won't come through. There is less butter in this recipe than in the Basic Biscuits because the cheese contains fat. Serve these as you would the Basic Biscuits.

2 cups all-purpose flour

4 teaspoons baking powder

1 teaspoon salt

6 tablespoons (⅔ stick) unsalted butter, very cold, cut into ½-inch pieces

¾ cup grated sharp cheddar cheese

¾ cup milk

Melted butter, for brushing (optional)

Flour, for dusting (optional)

Preheat the oven to 400° F.

Combine the flour, baking powder, and salt in a mixing bowl. Add the butter to the flour mixture. Work it quickly with your fingertips, breaking up the butter into smaller pieces, but leaving a few larger pieces than you think you should—to make the biscuits buttery.

Add the cheddar to the bowl and stir it in.

Add the milk to the bowl and stir it in with a spoon to make a moist but not sticky dough. It should be dry enough to roll.

Flour a work surface and place the dough on it. Sprinkle the dough with a little flour and roll it out to about ¾ inch thick. Dust off the top and fold it in thirds. Roll it out again ¾ inch thick, or if making miniature biscuits, roll out the dough to ½ inch thick. Cut out the biscuits in any size you like. Place the biscuits on a greased baking sheet and either brush them with melted butter, dust them lightly with flour, or do nothing at all. If you want soft-sided biscuits, arrange them so that their sides are touching; otherwise, space them an inch or two apart. Bake them for about 15 minutes, until they have risen and are lightly browned.

Yield: 10 to 12 3-inch biscuits

NOTE: These are best eaten right out of the oven.

Ham and Black Pepper Biscuits

Here is yet another biscuit variation. The ham and pepper in this version add a complexity that should be considered when matching them to an entrée. Choose a simpler entrée, one not so highly seasoned that they compete. For example, while a plain or corn biscuit would complement a gumbo nicely, providing a mild contrast to the spice of the stew, this ham and pepper biscuit would just add more of the same flavors. With fried chicken or fish, however, it would be great.

If you happen to have an end from a country ham, too small to do much with, here is the perfect use for it. Obviously, the better the ham, the better these biscuits will be. Also, if using a particularly salty ham, cut back on the salt in the recipe a bit.

2 cups all-purpose flour

4 teaspoons baking powder

¾ teaspoon salt

7 tablespoons unsalted butter, very cold, cut into ½-inch pieces

¼ pound ham, coarsely chopped

Approximately 8 grinds of black pepper

¾ cup milk

Preheat the oven to 400° F.

Combine the flour, baking powder, and salt in a mixing bowl. Add the butter to the flour mixture. Work it quickly with your fingertips, breaking up the butter into smaller pieces. Leave a few pieces larger than you think you should—these will form nice buttery pockets in the biscuits. Add the ham and pepper to the bowl and stir them in with a spoon.

Add the milk to the bowl and stir it in. The dough should be wet but not too sticky—it should be rollable.

Flour a work surface and turn the dough out onto it. Sprinkle the dough with a little flour and roll it out to about ¾ inch thick. Dust off the top and fold it in thirds. Roll it out again ¾ inch thick or, if making miniature biscuits, to ½ inch thick. Cut the dough into any size biscuits you want.

Place the biscuits on a greased baking sheet. If you like, you may brush the tops with melted butter and sprinkle them lightly with more pepper. For crispier biscuits, space them 1 or 2 inches apart. For softer ones, crowd them so that their sides are touching. Bake the biscuits for about 15 minutes, until they have risen and are lightly browned. Serve hot.

Yield: 10 to 12 3-inch biscuits

Popovers

These are just right with roast beef or stews. Their prodigal puff is irresistible. You can vary them by sprinkling the tops with poppy seeds, herbs, Parmesan, or chopped scallion. For the best rise, use a special popover tin. A muffin tin can also be used, but the popovers will have a squatter shape.

4 eggs	1¾ cups all-purpose flour
1¾ cups milk	Poppy seeds, chopped fresh herbs,
½ teaspoon salt	grated Parmesan, or chopped
2 tablespoons unsalted butter,	scallions as garnish (optional)
melted	

Combine the eggs, milk, salt, and melted butter in a medium bowl and whisk well to combine. Add the flour and whisk just enough to form a fairly smooth batter. It should be the consistency of heavy cream.

Pour the batter into a well-greased or nonstick popover pan. Be sure to fill the compartments only halfway; if you overfill them, the popovers will not be airy inside. Sprinkle lightly with any of the garnishes, if desired.

Place the popover pan in a cold oven. Turn the oven to 425° F. Bake the popovers until puffed well over the rim and golden brown, 25 to 35 minutes. Serve immediately.

Yield: 1 dozen popovers

Feather Dumplings

I found this recipe in my grandmother's personal recipe book and tried it out. These are light fluffy dumplings that are steamed directly on top of simmering stew. You can also make them in a separate pot in some simmering chicken stock and serve them alongside a plate of greens or sautéed mixed vegetables for a satisfying meal.

The dumplings are best eaten right away, but I have also removed them from the pot to a bowl and held them at room temperature for a few hours. I steam them over water for a few minutes to reheat.

1 cup all-purpose flour	1 egg
2½ teaspoons baking powder	½ cup milk
½ teaspoon salt	

Place the flour, baking powder, and salt in a mixing bowl and whisk to blend.

In another bowl, beat together the egg and milk. Add them to the dry ingredients and whisk until smooth. Do not overmix.

Drop the batter by the tablespoonful into lightly simmering stew or stock, leaving a little room around each dumpling. The batter will at least double in size. Cover the pot immediately and steam the dumplings for exactly 15 minutes—no peeking!

Remove the dumplings from the pot with a slotted spoon and serve them on the plate nestled up to the stew.

Yield: 4 servings

Texas Toast

When I first saw a description of Texas Toast, my taste buds stood at attention. This preparation conjures up images of campfires, cowboys, and chuck wagons. It's the kind of food considered sinful by the PC police, but can be immensely enjoyed by outlaws.

Texas Toast is meant to be part of a panfried steak dinner, but I see no reason not to prepare it with pork chops, venison, or sautéed duck breasts.

To give exact measurements in this recipe would be to go against the spirit, the essence of the thing, so toss aside your inhibitions and go wild!

2 slices home-style white bread or	Chili powder to taste
4 slices Italian bread	Salt to taste
Garlic powder to taste	Cayenne pepper to taste

Fry a steak. Pour off all but about ¼ cup of the fat in the pan.

Sprinkle the bread on both sides with the garlic powder, chili powder, salt, and cayenne. Add the bread to the fat in the pan, and fry it on both sides until golden. Serve it on the plate next to your steak so it can soak up the meat juices.

Yield: 2 servings

NOTE: A campfire greatly enhances the flavor of Texas Toast.

Parmesan Twists

This is basically a pizza dough, cut and rolled in Parmesan cheese. Parmesan Twists are delicious with soups made from vegetables or meats.

1¼ teaspoons active dry yeast

½ cup water

Pinch of sugar

1 teaspoon salt

2 teaspoons olive oil, plus more for brushing

¼ cup plus 2 tablespoons cornmeal

Approximately 2 cups all-purpose flour

¾ cup grated Parmesan

Poppy seeds (optional)

Combine the yeast, water, and sugar in a bowl and let stand a few minutes until the yeast has dissolved.

Add the salt, 2 teaspoons of olive oil, and ¼ cup of cornmeal to the yeast mixture and stir to combine. Add the flour, ¼ cup at a time, stirring with a spoon. When the dough becomes too stiff to stir with a spoon, use your hands. Add enough flour to form a kneadable dough.

Turn the dough out onto a floured surface and knead it until it is smooth and elastic.

Place a little olive oil in a large bowl and place the dough in it. Turn the dough to coat it with the olive oil and then cover the bowl with plastic wrap or a towel. Place it in a warm spot and let the dough rise until doubled in bulk, 1 to 1½ hours.

Preheat the oven to 425°F.

Punch the dough down with your fist to release the gases that have built up. Place the dough on a work surface and flatten it with your hands. Cut it into 12 equal pieces.

Place the remaining 2 tablespoons of cornmeal on one dinner plate and the Parmesan on another. With your fingertips, roll a piece of dough to form a rope about 9 inches long and ¾ inch thick. Brush the rope with olive oil, roll it in the cornmeal, and then in the Parmesan. Twist it and then lay it on a baking sheet. Sprinkle with poppy seeds if you wish. Repeat with the rest of the dough and then bake the twists for about 15 minutes, until puffed and browned.

Yield: about 12 twists

NOTE: Serve as soon as possible—they don't keep overnight.

Corn-Chili Crackers

These delicious crackers are enjoyable with soups and stews. They can be cut out with any small cookie cutter you like (I use a little duck and make quackers) or cut into squares with a knife. They keep well in an airtight container.

¼ cup yellow cornmeal

¼ cup all-purpose flour

½ teaspoon baking powder

¼ teaspoon salt, plus more for sprinkling

⅛ teaspoon ground cumin

½ teaspoon chili powder, plus more for dusting

1 tablespoon unsalted butter, cut into small bits

2 to 3 tablespoons milk

Preheat the oven to 450° F.

Combine the cornmeal, flour, baking powder, ¼ teaspoon salt, cumin, and ½ teaspoon chili powder in a medium bowl. Add the butter and work it in a bit with your fingertips.

Stir in 2 tablespoons of the milk to form a dough. It should be wet enough to just hold together but not too wet to roll out. If necessary, add the other tablespoon of milk.

Roll out the dough on a lightly floured work surface to ⅛ inch thick. Use a cookie cutter to cut out the crackers and place them on a lightly buttered sheet pan. Lightly sprinkle with salt and chili powder and bake until lightly browned, about 7 minutes. Cool before serving.

Yield: about 15 crackers

Poppy-Oat Crackers

Oats give these crackers a bit more earthiness. You can try sesame seeds instead of poppy seeds or a combination of both for variation.

2 tablespoons rolled oats

½ cup all-purpose flour

¼ teaspoon baking powder

⅓ teaspoon salt

¼ teaspoon sugar

½ teaspoon poppy seeds

1 tablespoon unsalted butter, cut
   into little pieces

1 tablespoon milk, plus more for
   brushing

1 to 2 tablespoons water

Preheat the oven to 450° F.

Place the oats in a blender and pulse them quickly until they are coarsely ground. Put the ground oats in a medium bowl.

Add the flour, baking powder, salt, sugar, and ¼ teaspoon of the poppy seeds. Add the butter and work it in a bit with your fingers.

Stir in 1 tablespoon of the milk and 1 tablespoon of the water to form a dough. Add the remaining tablespoon of water if the dough is not holding together. It should be just damp enough to form a ball, but not too wet to roll.

Roll out the dough on a lightly floured work surface to ⅛ inch thick. Fold the dough in thirds and then roll it out again ⅛ inch thick. Cut out the crackers and brush them very lightly with milk. Sprinkle with the remaining ¼ teaspoon of poppy seeds. Place the crackers on a lightly buttered sheet pan and bake until lightly browned, about 7 minutes. Let cool before eating. Store in an airtight container.

Yield: about 15 crackers

Sesame Crackers

I like to use a combination of white and black sesame seeds for these crackers. Black sesame seeds can be found in Asian markets.

½ cup all-purpose flour	1 teaspoon white or black sesame
1 tablespoon cornmeal	seeds
¼ teaspoon baking powder	1 tablespoon unsalted butter, cut
½ teaspoon sugar	into little pieces
½ teaspoon salt	2 to 3 tablespoons milk, plus more
	for brushing

Preheat the oven to 450° F.

Place the flour, cornmeal, baking powder, sugar, salt, and ½ teaspoon of the sesame seeds in a medium bowl. Stir to combine. Add the butter and work it in a little with your fingertips.

Stir in 2 tablespoons of milk to form a dough. If it does not just hold together in a ball, add the last tablespoon of milk. Roll out the dough on a lightly floured work surface to ⅛ inch thick. Fold the dough over in thirds and then roll it out again ⅛ inch thick. Cut out the crackers and then brush them very lightly with milk. Sprinkle with the remaining sesame seeds.

Place the crackers on a lightly buttered sheet pan and bake them until lightly browned, about 7 minutes. Cool completely before serving. Store in an airtight container.

Yield: about 15 crackers

Cheese Straws

These are so good they are almost hedonistic. Use the sharpest cheddar you can find—run-of-the-mill supermarket cheddar is too bland and greasy. You can make the dough and refrigerate it, cutting off and baking what you need. It keeps 2 weeks this way.

8 ounces sharp cheddar cheese

3 tablespoons unsalted butter, softened

¾ teaspoon powdered, mustard, preferably Colman's

5 dashes Worcestershire sauce

¼ teaspoon salt

¼ teaspoon cayenne pepper

½ cup plus 2 tablespoons all-purpose flour

Sweet paprika, for dusting

Preheat the oven to 425°F.

Grate the cheddar using the small holes on your grater. Place the grated cheddar in a medium mixing bowl with the butter, mustard, Worcestershire, salt, and cayenne. Cream everything together well.

Add the flour and mix until a workable dough is formed. Break off pieces of about tablespoon size and, using your fingers (remember your Play-Doh years), roll the dough out into a rope about ¼ inch thick and 8 inches long. When rolling, start in the center and work your fingers out toward the ends. Place the rope off to one side while you continue with the rest of the dough.

Gently flatten the ropes a bit and dust them lightly with paprika. Place the Cheese Straws on a sheet pan and bake them until lightly browned, about 8 minutes. Remove the straws from the sheet pan and let them cool on a rack.

Yield: about 20 straws

Goat Cheese Toasts

Touches like this can transform a simple soup into something special. Try these on vegetable purée soups, especially tomato.

4 ounces soft goat cheese, Montrachet style, at room temperature	**½ teaspoon minced garlic**
	4 grinds of black pepper
	2 teaspoons finely cut fresh chives
1 egg yolk	**8 melba toast rounds**

Preheat the oven to 425°F.

Place the goat cheese, egg yolk, garlic, pepper, and chives in a mixing bowl. Using a wooden spoon, thoroughly combine the ingredients.

Spread about 1 teaspoon of goat cheese mixture on each melba toast round, mounding it in the middle.

Place the cheese toasts on a sheet pan and bake until the cheese is hot, about 5 minutes. Watch the toasts to make sure they don't burn—if they are cooking too fast, lower the temperature.

Carefully float the Goat Cheese Toasts on top of individual servings of soup and serve immediately.

Yield: 4 servings

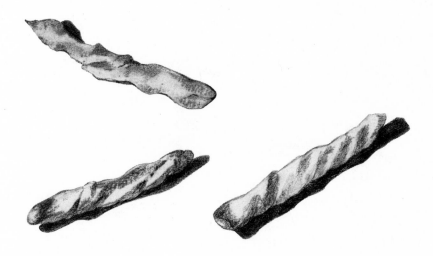

Lagniappe

Béchamel Sauce

◆

Barbecue Powder

◆

Tart Pastry

◆

Whole Wheat Pastry

◆

Herb Butter

◆

Chili Butter

Béchamel Sauce

This recipe makes a thick béchamel, which is good for creamed dishes in which the vegetable gives off liquid, thereby thinning the sauce. It contains no salt and pepper because the seasoning can be added to the final dish.

3 tablespoons unsalted butter	**1 whole clove**
3 tablespoons all-purpose flour	**1 small onion, peeled**
2 cups milk	

In a small, nonreactive saucepan, melt the butter over low heat. Add the flour and whisk well. Cook the roux very gently, whisking often, until it starts to give off a slightly nutty aroma, about 3 minutes. Be careful not to brown it.

Add a bit of the milk to the roux, whisking well to prevent lumps. When it is incorporated and a paste has formed, add a bit more, and whisk again. Add the rest of the milk, whisking vigorously.

Stick the clove into the onion and add them to the sauce. Simmer the sauce very gently, whisking often, until it no longer tastes floury, about 15 minutes. Strain the béchamel, discarding the onion.

Yield: about 2 cups

NOTE: The sauce can be made several days ahead of time. To store, press plastic wrap directly onto the surface of the sauce to prevent a skin from forming and refrigerate.

Barbecue Powder

This recipe will make more spice mix than you need for 1 batch of fries, but you can store it indefinitely in your spice rack. It's also delicious as a seasoning for steak, pork, chicken, Cornish hens, squab, or quail.

1 tablespoon cayenne pepper	2 tablespoons salt
2 tablespoons chili powder	4 teaspoons garlic powder
4 teaspoons sweet paprika	4 teaspoons sugar

Put all the ingredients in a mixing bowl and stir to combine. Transfer to a jar and cover tightly.

Tart Pastry

1½ cups all-purpose flour	½ teaspoon salt
¼ cup (½ stick) unsalted butter,	1 egg yolk
cut into small pieces	3 to 4 tablespoons ice water

Place the flour, butter, and salt in a bowl. With your fingertips, rub in the butter until it resembles coarse meal. Add the egg yolk and 3 tablespoons of the water and mix with your hands. If the dough is too dry, add some more water; it should just hold together. Form the dough into a ball and then flatten it into a disk. Wrap it in plastic wrap and let it rest, refrigerated, for at least 1 hour (overnight is better) before rolling.

Yield: 1 9- to 10-inch pastry shell

Whole Wheat Pastry

Whole wheat pastry adds a bit of rusticity to a tart and is nice with more assertive vegetables like tomatoes or eggplant.

1 cup all-purpose flour

1 cup whole wheat pastry flour

Pinch of salt

7 tablespoons unsalted butter, very cold, cut into bits

3 to 4 tablespoons ice water

Place the all-purpose and whole wheat flours in a mixing bowl with the salt. Stir to combine. Add the butter and work it in with your fingertips or a pastry blender until it is in pea-sized nuggets.

Stir the ice water into the mixture, a tablespoon at a time, until the pastry forms a ball. Don't mix the dough any more than necessary to achieve this. Form the pastry into a disk and wrap it in plastic. Refrigerate it for at least one hour before rolling.

Yield: enough for 1 9- or 10-inch shell

Herb Butter

Herb butter is a good thing to have around the house. You can roll it into a log, wrapped in foil, and keep it in the freezer until needed. Just slice off the desired quantity and return the rest to the freezer. Herb butter comes in handy for tossing with boiled noodles, melting on potatoes, spreading on biscuits, or mixing with steamed vegetables.

½ cup (1 stick) unsalted butter, softened

1 tablespoon finely cut fresh chives

½ teaspoon minced fresh thyme

¼ teaspoon minced fresh tarragon, chervil, and/or mint

2 teaspoons minced shallot or scallion

Salt and freshly ground pepper to taste

Squeeze of fresh lemon juice

Place the butter in a mixing bowl and add the chives, thyme, tarragon, shallot, salt and pepper, and lemon juice. Cream everything together thoroughly. Taste for seasonings and adjust. Use immediately or store in the refrigerator or freezer.

Yield: about 8 portions

Chili Butter

Although this butter is intended for potatoes in this context, it is also delicious on chicken, pork, steak, and fish such as mako, tuna, or swordfish.

Chili Butter can be made ahead and then rolled into a cylinder with aluminum foil and refrigerated or frozen. When needed, just peel back the foil, slice as much as you need (which can be used immediately if sliced $\frac{1}{8}$ inch thick), rewrap, and return to the freezer.

I have used a dried poblano chili here, but a variety of chilis would work—decide for yourself how spicy you would like the butter. Chipotles—which are smoked, dried, ripe jalapeños—are excellent.

1 dried poblano chili	1 shallot, peeled and cut in
$\frac{1}{2}$ cup (1 stick) unsalted butter,	quarters
softened	Salt to taste
Juice of $\frac{1}{2}$ lemon	

Soak the chili in warm water for 20 minutes. When it has softened, drain the chili and remove the stem. Open up the chili and remove and discard the seeds. Tear the chili into large pieces.

Put the chili pieces, butter, lemon juice, shallot, and salt into a blender or food processor. Process until well blended. Use immediately or wrap in foil and store in the refrigerator or freezer.

Yield: enough for 8 baked potatoes

Index

Conversion Chart

Equivalent Imperial and Metric Measurements

American cooks use standard containers, the 8-ounce cup and a tablespoon that takes exactly 16 level fillings to fill that cup level. Measuring by cup makes it very difficult to give weight equivalents, as a cup of densely packed butter will weigh considerably more than a cup of flour. The easiest way therefore to deal with cup measurements in recipes is to take the amount by volume rather than by weight. Thus the equation reads:

1 cup = 240 ml = 8 fl. oz.   ½ cup = 120 ml = 4 fl. oz.

It is possible to buy a set of American cup measures in major stores around the world.

In the States, butter is often measured in sticks. One stick is the equivalent of 8 tablespoons. One tablespoon of butter is therefore the equivalent to ½ ounce / 15 grams.

LIQUID MEASURES

Fluid Ounces	U.S.	Imperial	Milliliters
	1 teaspoon	1 teaspoon	4
¼	2 teaspoons	1 dessertspoon	7
½	1 tablespoon	1 tablespoon	14
1	2 tablespoons	2 tablespoons	28
2	¼ cup	4 tablespoons	56
4	½ cup		110
5		¼ pint or 1 gill	140
6	¾ cup		170
8	1 cup		225
9			250, ¼ liter
10	1¼ cups	½ pint	280
12	1½ cups		340
15		¾ pint	420
16	2 cups		450
18	2¼ cups		500, ½ liter
20	2½ cups	1 pint	560
24	3 cups		675
25		1¼ pints	700
27	3½ cups		750
30	3¾ cups	1½ pints	840
32	4 cups or 1 quart		900
35		1¾ pints	980
36	4½ cups		1000, 1 liter
40	5 cups	2 pints or 1 quart	1120
48	6 cups		1350
50		2½ pints	1400
60	7½ cups	3 pints	1680
64	8 cups or 2 quarts		1800
72	9 cups		2000, 2 liters

SOLID MEASURES

U.S. and Imperial		Metric	
Ounces	Pounds	Grams	Kilos
1		28	
2		56	
3½		100	
4	¼	112	
5		140	
6		168	
8	½	225	
9		250	¼
12	¾	340	
16	1	450	
18		500	½
20	1¼	560	
24	1½	675	
27		750	¾
28	1¾	780	
32	2	900	
36	2¼	1000	1
40	2½	1100	
48	3	1350	
54		1500	1½
64	4	1800	
72	4½	2000	2
80	5	2250	2¼
90		2500	2½
100	6	2800	2¾

OVEN TEMPERATURE EQUIVALENTS

Fahrenheit	Celsius	Gas Mark	Description
225	110	¼	Cool
250	130	½	
275	140	1	Very Slow
300	150	2	
325	170	3	Slow
350	180	4	Moderate
375	190	5	
400	200	6	Moderately Hot
425	220	7	Fairly Hot
450	230	8	Hot
475	240	9	Very Hot
500	250	10	Extremely Hot

Any broiling recipes can be used with the grill of the oven, but beware of high-temperature grills.

EQUIVALENTS FOR INGREDIENTS

all-purpose flour—plain flour
arugula—rocket
baking sheet—oven tray
buttermilk—ordinary milk
cheesecloth—muslin
coarse salt—kitchen salt
confectioners' sugar—icing sugar
cornstarch—cornflour

eggplant—aubergine
granulated sugar—caster sugar
half and half—12% fat milk
heavy cream—double cream
light cream—single cream
lima beans—broad beans
parchment paper—greaseproof paper
plastic wrap—cling film

scallion—spring onion
sour cherry—morello cherry
unbleached flour—strong, white flour
vanilla bean—vanilla pod
zest—rind
zucchini—courgettes or marrow